THE SPIRIT OF CHRISTMAS

CREATIVE HOLIDAY IDEAS
BOOK FIFTEEN

The season of love, hope, joy, and peace, Christmas calls us into action, striving to make this much-anticipated occasion more meaningful and memorable for those we hold dear. Glowing lights, fragrant trees, majestic angels, dazzling ornaments, and colorfully wrapped packages delight all who see them, as do the tastes and aromas of fresh, home-cooked treats. This handy book has it all — beautiful decorations that anyone can make, creative gift ideas to please everyone, and mouth-watering recipes that will draw you and yours closer to the spirit and magic of Christmas. With this irresistible volume as your guide, you'll find it easier than ever to express the joy of the day, as well as the love we have for one another at this special time.

LEISURE ARTS, INC.
Little Rock, Arkansas

THE SPIRIT OF CHRISTMAS

BOOK FIFTEEN

EDITORIAL STAFF

Vice President and Editor-at-Large: Anne Van Wagner Childs
Vice President and Editor-in-Chief: Sandra Graham Case
Design Director: Cyndi Hansen
Editorial Director: Susan Frantz Wiles
Publications Director: Kristine Anderson Mertes
Creative Art Director: Gloria Bearden
Photography Director: Karen Hall
Art Operations Director: Jeff Curtis

DESIGN
Designers: Polly Tullis Browning, Diana Sanders Cates,
   Cherece Athy Cooper, Peggy Elliott Cunningham,
   Anne Pulliam Stocks, Linda Diehl Tiano, and Becky Werle
Executive Assistant: Debra Smith
Production Assistant: Karla Edgar

FOODS
Foods Editor: Jane Kenner Prather

OXMOOR HOUSE
Senior Foods Editor: Susan Carlisle Payne
Foods Editor: Kelly Hooper Troiano
Assistant Foods Editors: Rebecca C. Dopson and Julie Gunter
Copy Editor: Donna Baldone
Editorial Assistant: Jane E. Lorberau
Senior Designer: Melissa M. Clark
Crafts Editor: Catherine Corbett Fowler
Publishing Systems Administrator: Rick Tucker
Production Manager: Larry Hunter
Photographers: Jim Bathie and Brit Huckabay
Photography Stylist: Kay Clarke
Test Kitchen Director: Elizabeth Tyler Luckett
Test Kitchen Assistant Director: Julie Christopher
Test Kitchen Recipe Editor: Gayle Hays Sadler
Test Kitchen Staff: Gretchen Feldtman, R.D.; Jan A. Smith;
   David C. Gallent; Ana Price Kelly; and Jennifer A. Cofield

TECHNICAL
Managing Editor: Leslie Schick Gorrell
Technical Writers: Sherry Solida Ford and Theresa Hicks Young
Copy Editor: K.J. Smith
Technical Associate: Jennifer Potts Hutchings

EDITORIAL
Managing Editor: Suzie Puckett
Senior Associate Editor: Jennifer L. Riley
Associate Editor: Susan McManus Johnson

ART
Art Director: Mark Hawkins
Senior Production Artist and Color Technician: Mark R. Potter
Production Artists: Elaine Barry, Shalana Fleetwood, Clint Hanson,
   Faith Lloyd, Lora Puls, Rhonda Shelby, and Dana Vaughn
Staff Photographer: Russell Ganser
Photography Stylists: Tiffany Huffman and Janna Laughlin
Publishing Systems Administrator: Becky Riddle
Publishing Systems Assistants: Myra S. Means and
   Chris Wertenberger

PROMOTIONS
Associate Editor: Steven M. Cooper
Designer: Dale Rowett
Graphic Artist: Deborah Kelly

*"...and it was always said of him, that he knew how
to keep Christmas well, if any man alive possessed the
knowledge. May that be truly said of us, and all of us!"*

— From *A Christmas Carol* by Charles Dickens

BUSINESS STAFF

Publisher: Rick Barton
Vice President, Finance: Tom Siebenmorgen
Director of Corporate Planning and Development:
   Laticia Mull Cornett
Vice President, Retail Marketing: Bob Humphrey
Vice President, Sales: Ray Shelgosh

Vice President, National Accounts: Pam Stebbins
Retail Marketing Director: Margaret Sweetin
Vice President, Operations: Jim Dittrich
Comptroller, Operations: Rob Thieme
Retail Customer Service Manager: Wanda Price
Print Production Manager: Fred F. Pruss

Library of Congress Catalog Card Number 98-65188
International Standard Book Number 1-57486-196-4

10   9   8   7   6   5   4   3   2   1

CONTENTS

THE SIGHTS OF CHRISTMAS
Page 6

CONTENTS

THE
SIGHTS
OF
CHRISTMAS

In an instant, a few festive trims can transport us to Christmas — the beloved season of joyful celebration. Whether you prefer a sense of dreamy romance, natural elegance, or homespun country charm, you'll find plenty of innovative ideas in this Yuletide collection. Pick and choose from an exciting extravaganza of wreaths, stockings, ornaments, and other terrific trims to put a novel twist on traditional decorations or to create an enchanting new look for your holiday home.

EARTHLY GRANDEUR

Greet the holidays with the timeless grandeur of scarlet berries and velvety moss decorations. Arrayed in the vibrant colors of Christmas and emanating an earthy richness, these jewels of nature are ideal for dressing your entryway in style. Luxurious looking and easy to keep fresh, this display of subtle sophistication will dazzle guests all season long!

Welcoming visitors with seasonal decorum, our Entryway Spray (shown on page 9) begins with a Canadian pine swag. Loosen a piece of grapevine from a wreath and coil it around the pine swag. Finish by gluing or wiring silk amaryllis flowers, artificial leaves, juniper sprigs, and berry sprigs to the grapevine.

Reflect the splendors of nature with an ornate topper for a gilded mirror. Simply coil grapevine (cut from a wreath) around an evergreen garland and embellish with artificial leaves, juniper, berry sprigs, and silk amaryllis blooms. Add "shine" with a few Seeded Star Ornaments, made by gluing rye grass seed onto papier-mâché stars and a star anise to one of the points.

Many of the same naturals used on our Mirror Accent decorate the Tabletop Topiaries and the Trio of Trees in weathered urns.

A pair of Stately Reindeer wear lush coats of sheet moss glued over their papier-mâché bodies. Create their regal red racks by cutting off the tops of the original antlers and inserting twigs and berry sprigs into the openings. To add more color, glue extra berries to the twigs.

Instructions for Earthly Grandeur are on page 114.

Winding its way heavenward, the Banister Roping is a longer version of the Mirror Accent shown on page 10.

A Natural Candle Arrangement of pillars clustered atop a moss-covered base is a delightful accent for an earthy entryway.

Even your most humble presentations will be well received when encased in moss and decorated with glued-on twigs, berry sprigs, star anise, Seeded Star Ornaments, and strips of reindeer moss. To cover gift boxes with velvety moss, brush a mixture of 2 parts craft glue to 1 part water onto the lids and sides (working on one small area at a time), then press a layer of moss sheeting over the glue. Enliven packages wrapped in pretty paper with more naturals and ribbons. See page 155 for tips on making remarkable bows.

Instructions for Earthly Grandeur are on page 114.

FRUITFUL OPULENCE

Celebrate the season of our most bountiful blessings with a tasteful arrangement of frosted faux fruits and glistening fabrics. Luxuriously displayed on your tree, mantel, and tabletops, these irresistible riches will infuse your home with the opulence that stems from applauding nature's grandest offerings.

Let your decorations be fruitful, and you'll multiply the joy in your home! For a tree (shown on page 14) that's the cream of the holiday crop, first add a garland heavy with frosted faux fruits. Then refine the opulent look by nestling miniature Fruit Topiaries (also shown opposite) among the branches and placing Framed Prints (page 14) here and there. Next use copper and gold ribbons, glittery beads, tassels, glass ornaments, and berry sprigs to create generous layers of richness. Top off the tree with a bountiful "corsage" (this page, top) arranged using fruit clusters and loops of iridescent ribbon. Your finished Christmas conifer will verily float above the festivities on a cloud of coppery skirting!

To create an Opulent Mirror Accent (opposite), interlace garland greenery with ribbons and other trims. Enhance the setting with a Fruitful Mantelscape featuring billows of shimmery fabric beneath a buffet of fruits and frills; anchor each end with a Bountiful Topiary.

Once the rest of the house is dressed in all its glory, relax in the merry light of a Fruitful Table Wreath (this page, bottom). Simply arrange choice fruit and greenery picks on a grapevine wreath, using hot glue and floral wire to hold them in place; then weave in a string of glistening beads and some berry sprigs. Complete the centerpiece with a golden candle in a hurricane globe.

Instructions for Fruitful Opulence are on page 116.

NOBLE ESTATE

Spruce up your home with the genteel prestige of a noble country estate. Stately shields, majestic fowl, and golden stalks of grain will evoke a sense of heritage while refining your vision of the holidays. This handsome presentation radiates traditional family values.

Groom a regal "family tree" (shown on page 18) with our Shield and Faux-Leather Ornaments. Pheasant feathers and rye stalks create an attractive topper and add fullness to the branches. Spatter-painted papier-mâché eggs in Feather Wreaths are nestled here and there, reflecting the delicate touch of nature. Ornaments matching those on the tree can also be used to give distinction to presents wrapped in traditional plaid paper.

Take advantage of the season's quieter moments by relaxing in the comfort of a princely Fleece Throw With Gilded Shield (above). Soften the memories with a cozy combo of Aristocratic Pillows.

Let a Trio of Wild Geese (opposite) preen themselves above the fireplace by arranging pheasant feathers, rye stalks, silk poinsettias, and assorted berries in ceramic geese planters. Accent the mantel with bright red tapers placed in handsome Faux-Leather Candlesticks. Plaid Stockings make a nice finishing touch.

Instructions for Noble Estate begin on page 118.

DREAMY WHITE CHRISTMAS

Bring the dreamy romance of a winter wonderland to your home this year by decorating in snowy shades of white. Shimmering trims combined with the soft glow of candlelight will add elegance and warmth to seasonal activities and intimate gatherings.

Holiday enchantment will fill the air as you tuck fancy treasures into these Stunning Stockings (opposite). The warm glow from the Illuminated Mantelscape will invite all to gather 'round and entertain dreams of a white Christmas. Lined with linen, the mantel blooms with garland greens and preserved gardenias. Assorted candlesticks add height to the arrangement and cast soft light onto the classy Winter Berry Wreath.

Trim the tree to complement your impressive mantel. Fill small wire baskets with Spanish moss and top with dried hydrangea sprigs. Cover a small grapevine wreath with tallow berries and finish with a white ribbon bow. Glue white buttons over a plastic foam ball; then pin a length of thin silver braid to the ball and tie the ends into a bow. Enhance ordinary tree lights by covering some of the bulbs with purchased frosty globes.

Instructions for Dreamy White Christmas are on page 124.

Add a polished touch to the tree with a Delicate Topper made from a wispy bow, bits of faux greenery, and a preserved gardenia. (See Bows on page 155.)

Our wonderful Wintry Packages will make the scene under your tree look as spectacular as the evergreen itself. Be inventive, and use your creative flair to make coordinating tags and other decorations for gift bags and boxes. Dress up larger bags by punching holes along the top edge and weaving an organdy ribbon through them; tie the streamers into an elegant bow. For a joy-filled carrier, add ribbon handles by punching two holes on each side of a bag, near the top; thread the ends of a length of ribbon through the holes, knotting them inside. Finish by tying the tops of the handles together with a third length of ribbon. Accent other gifts with preserved gardenia blossoms or a few sprigs of glittery artificial greenery cut from a garland. Don't be surprised if recipients say these packages are too gorgeous to open!

Welcome guests to the wintry panorama of your living room with this dazzling Holiday Swag gracing the entrance. To construct it, wire a fruit-laden garland to an evergreen garland and entwine ribbon throughout. Drape over the doorway and allow to cascade down the sides.

Instructions for Dreamy White Christmas are on page 124.

For a holiday table setting that's as magnificent as the rest of your décor, craft a version of our Radiant Centerpiece (opposite). Begin by cutting a block of floral foam in half; then place one piece on each side of a floral foam wreath. Cover the foam with evergreen picks and pieces cut from a tree garland. Refine the effect by placing a large candle in the center and arranging assorted height candlesticks among the spread.

Augment the table's crowning glory with these fabulous Chairback Decorations (this page, top). Form by wiring a length of frosty fruit garland to another garland of artificial greenery and interweaving two strands of silk ribbon throughout. (Use a string or fabric measuring tape to quickly determine the length needed to create a suitable drape for your chair style.) Tie the arrangement to the chairback with lengths of wire-edged ribbon.

Add style to your white linen napkins with a Napkin Ring tied using silk-trimmed organdy ribbon. Glue a preserved gardenia blossom to each ribbon ring.

Instructions for Dreamy White Christmas are on page 124.

A STERLING YULETIDE TEA

Serve up a refreshing Yuletide this year with trims reminiscent of an old-fashioned afternoon tea. Classic red-and-white china, polished silver, silk roses, and elegant angels dressed in toile de jouy combine to create a setting that's ideal for sharing a cup of tea and warm conversation. This eloquent décor sparkles with sterling holiday charm!

Dish out a generous helping of holiday cheer for your family and friends to enjoy by decorating your Christmas tree with colorful dinnerware, plaid bows, and red silk roses! Foster warm thoughts by nestling sheet moss, greenery, and silk rosebuds in dainty Trimmed Teacups and dangling them from ribbon bows looped through the handles. Sweeten the scene with an assortment of Berry-Adorned Saucers. Simply mount a plate hanger on each saucer, twist and tape together the stems of two berry picks, and finish by gluing the stems to the back of the plate and bending the berries over to the front. Continue feeding the Christmas spirit with gleaming Silverware Icicles, made by gluing ribbon bows to the ends of forks, spoons, and knives and attaching hangers. Fabric Rose Ornaments, Tasseled "Frog" Ornaments, and Charming Angels balance out the tasteful look. Best of all, when the season is over, you can disassemble your creations and return the china and flatware to the cupboard!

Displayed near the tree's twinkling lights, a shining silver tea service (opposite, top) will reflect the holiday joy around you.

Just as a special tablecloth can highlight stunning place settings, a graceful Layered Tree Skirt (opposite, bottom) will set off the china adornments on your tree. Enhance the scene even more with a romantic collection of packages wrapped in rose-print paper.

Instructions for A Sterling Yuletide Tea begin on page 125.

Proclaim good tidings with a Roses and Angels Wreath above the mantel. To craft the heavenly decoration, attach artificial greenery, berries, silk roses, and ribbons to an evergreen wreath. Wire on a pair of Charming Angels to finish. Add embellished tabs to create the gracefully swagged Mantel Scarf.

Add a little spice to your Christmas tearoom by displaying transferware platters (opposite, top left) and silver serving pieces throughout the room.

Light up a cozy sitting area with a "Christmas Tea" Lamp (opposite, top right) fashioned from a silver teapot.

Set a handsome drawer or box near the front door to hold one-of-a-kind Greeting Cards (opposite, bottom) that you make for hand-delivery to guests. Simply use ribbon to decorate a blank card along the fold or outside edge; then stamp a greeting inside the card and on the envelope. You can even add a shimmering satin frog from our Mantel Scarf. Keep priceless holiday pictures and stories alive for years to come in a fabric-covered Christmas Memories Journal.

Instructions for A Sterling Yuletide Tea begin on page 125.

WOODLAND HAVEN

Nestle in for the holidays with decorations inspired by a quiet woodland haven. This snow-frosted backdrop will help family members and special guests distance themselves from the chaotic rush of shopping and parties and allow them to begin savoring the gentle spirit of the season.

Placid tones of teal and tan cloak our Woodland Santa. He wisely holds a rustic staff to help him navigate the snowy landscape on his annual journey to deliver holiday goodwill.

While on his serene trek, Father Christmas may stop amidst gently falling snowflakes to watch various forest creatures gather food from nature's pantry. The Woodland Ornaments featured on our tree include delightfully detailed felt bunnies, acorns, and birds, as well as easy snowflakes and bird nests.

Appliqué some of the soft felt ornaments onto fabric pouches and use them to hold special gifts for family members. Place the hand-crafted Woodland Gift Bags under the evergreen for a special touch of charm.

Instructions for Woodland Haven begin on page 129.

Continue the pleasing timberland theme with Birdhouse Ornaments created by applying a birchbark finish to cardboard tubes.

A full-color chart makes it relaxing and enjoyable to cross stitch this loving pair of Christmas angels for your home. As you stitch "A Peaceful Christmastide," calmly reflect on the message of holiday joy these heavenly beings were sent to convey so many years ago.

Instructions for Woodland Haven begin on page 129.

This snow-frosted wreath shelters the promise of a Christmas that's in harmony with nature. Begin by lightly applying snow medium to preserved branches of salal leaves. While the leaves dry, apply glitter snow medium to pinecones and a twig wreath. Use hot glue and floral wire to attach the salal leaves, pinecones, silk poinsettias, a Wintry Nest ornament, and embroidered Woodland Ornaments to the wreath. Hang the lovely accent above the mantel to complete your home's restful garden look. Then sit back and unwind, knowing you've done your part to spread peace on earth this holiday season!

REINDEER GAMES

Let this herd of friendly reindeer entertain you with merriment and heartwarming fun while you await Santa's arrival. Children of all ages will jump for joy at the sight of your holiday tree covered with these playful homespun trims!

Let the games begin! Perched high atop the tree, our Friendly Posable Deer Topper holds his Primitive Gold Star Ornament high to guide Santa's sleigh safely to your home.

Appliquéd to our "En-deer-ing" Tree Skirt, these watchful reindeer will deter mischievous boys and girls from sneaking an early peek at their presents!

Fashion a Homespun Holiday Mantel (opposite) by entwining an evergreen garland with a string of miniature white lights and a length of dried naturals. Tuck in a pair of finial candlesticks, a few trims, and some Jingle Bell Ornaments made by sponge painting weathered bells white and attaching bows fashioned from chenille cording. Finish the cozy, country look by hanging up a pair of Homespun Stockings for St. Nick to fill on Christmas Eve.

Instructions for Reindeer Games begin on page 140.

Lead the way to the festivities by posting Primitive Gold Star and Whimsical Sign Ornaments on the evergreen. To make the playful signs, photocopy the patterns on page 143 onto card stock and mount them on corrugated craft cardboard. A Jolly Reindeer Ornament sports wire antlers and a bright button nose. When he needs to fuel up for more merrymaking, he can nibble on a Feed Cone Ornament.

Post this Christmas Laurel Wreath (opposite) in your home and give a Friendly Posable Deer Topper the honor of sitting in the winner's circle! Start by weaving a garland of pinecones, berries, and other naturals around an evergreen wreath. Then attach aged-iron jingle bells and Primitive Gold Star Ornaments with glue or wire.

Instructions for Reindeer Games begin on page 140.

DECORATING
MADE EASY

If you're wishing St. Nick would bring you a little extra time for decking the halls, then these easy decorating strategies are for you! Simply gather a few basic supplies, and you'll be surprised how quickly you can fill your home with cheer. Don't neglect items that are part of your everyday décor either — that china cabinet could be a stunning showcase for your Santa collection!

Measure out a little excitement for your family each day of the Christmas season with a Kitchen Advent Tree decorated with dried citrus fruits, cinnamon sticks, berries, and other naturals. From her spot atop the aromatic half-tree, a rustic angel follows the "recipe" from a handmade Advent Sign as she cooks up a heavenly mixture of Love, Hope, Joy, and Peace for your home. Children especially will enjoy the daily treat of choosing a new Advent Box from the Advent Basket to open and place on the evergreen.

Instructions for Decorating Made Easy are on page 148.

HELPFUL TIP:

For a tree that shimmers with tiny points of light, such as our Santa-filled tree on page 48, a good rule of thumb is to plan for 100 miniature lights for each foot of tree. (If you have a 7-foot tree, you will need 700 lights.) You may want more lights if your tree is fuller. To make your tree shine from within, wind lights clockwise around the trunk from the bottom to the top. Then wrap back down to the base of the top branch; continue wrapping each branch to its tip and back to the trunk as you move around the tree and down.

Nothing says "Merry Christmas!" quite like fancy bows and streamers of shimmering ribbon. Decorate your home with these dressy accents and you'll have a versatile backdrop for any holiday gathering. To spruce up your evergreen, simply gather an assortment of wire-edged ribbons in traditional shades of crimson and gold, and then let your imagination run free. In other words, get wild with ribbon! You can tie up a collection of Becoming Bow Ornaments just by using a different number of loops for each type of ribbon; add variety by dangling baubles from a few bows. (For tips on bow-making, see Bows, page 155.) Unroll more of the bright yardage to shape flowing garlands for the branches and a sensational Streamered Tree Topper. Purchased drapery tiebacks, ornaments, white lights, and mistletoe all make ideal flourishes for a timeless holiday package the whole family is sure to enjoy!

HELPFUL TIP:

To decorate a 7-foot tree, you will need 20 to 30 yards of each type of ribbon for garland. The tree topper bow requires about 10 yards. For all the small red bows on our tree, we used about 15 yards of ribbon. The medium bows of golden ribbon took about 20 yards.

Our Classic Christmas Centerpiece is a cinch to make using a plump pillar candle and bits of ribbon and other trims from the tree. Displayed on a shimmering bed of georgette, the eye-catching luminary will instill the room with a warm glow.

Instructions for Decorating Made Easy are on page 148.

THE SHARING OF CHRISTMAS

Out of the overflow of our hearts comes the desire to share the joy of the season with those we love. Whether you want to nurture your favorite gardener, round up a few goodies for a cowboy, feed a child's creativity, greet a dog lover, or treat a sweetheart, we have inspiring ideas for everyone on your holiday list. You'll also find attractive home accents, as well as quick and inexpensive gifts to share with coworkers and classmates. Best of all, these gifts will reflect your creativity and caring without a clue of how easy they were to do!

great idea for CRaFTy kids

Pleasing a budding crafter is as easy as packing a lunch. Just decorate a plastic lunch box with craft foam cutouts and fill with a rainbow of foam beads in fun shapes, plastic lacing, and child-safe scissors. The colorful kit will keep imaginative little minds and hands busy for hours stringing up friendship necklaces and bracelets!

Whether he's more comfortable in the saddle or in a recliner, your special cowpoke will stay home on the range to enjoy this flavorful basket! Rope one together by placing his favorite Tex-Mex munchies and a classic Western video in a bandanna-lined hat. Spice up the package with a few faux peppers before wrapping it with clear plastic and a concha tie.

wild west wrap-up

simply
homegrown

The cottage freshness of this Gardener's Window Box (page 150) will have plant lovers seeing visions of spring blooms! Sow the seeds for this botanical bouquet by placing a block of floral foam in an ivy-stamped wooden box, leaving room to "plant" a small potted daisy. Cover the foam with moss and arrange gardening tools, gloves, and packets of flower seeds around an outdoor figurine. Tuck in a cushy kneeling pad to complete the thoughtful package.

for bathing
beauties

Help a lovely lady escape her daily demands for a while with a luxurious pack of bath gadgets, soaps, and lotions. Created by wiring an ivy wreath to one of grapevine and attaching artificial flowers, the powder room accent comes full circle with the addition of lacy bath bead bundles and a feminine bow.

for pampered pups

Toss your dog more than a bone this Noel ... give him a Super Simple Dog Bed (page 150) stuffed with doghouse comforts. Tail wags and canine kisses will abound when Puppy unties the ribbon on a slew of chews in a new bowl! After the excitement wears off, pamper your pet with his new brush. Then take a picture of him sporting his Christmas collar to display in the Best Friend's Frame (page 150)! You can even personalize his bowl and brush with paint pens.

it's a sweet treat

Treat someone nice to a doubly sweet gift by decorating a jar of cinnamon disks with a Festive Floral Topper (page 151) and candy "berries." A simple gingham bow finishes the look for a charming holiday accent that's fun to dip into!

a box to
treasure

Destined to be the jewel of the vanity, this Bead-Embellished Box (page 151) is a perfect gift for a lady who's precious to you. She'll treasure its elegant charm and appreciate having a place to deposit her rings and other valuables while she showers or sleeps.

twinkle, twinkle, little star

Show your coworkers and fellow group members you're thinking of them by filling plastic cups with goodies and wrapping them in clear plastic bags. Dress up each quick & easy gift in a twinkling with a wire-star garland, ribbon, and a handmade tag.

a time to give

The time is ripe for gifting others! Bestow our classic Decoupaged Clock (page 152) on anyone who appreciates tasteful home accents. The soothing motion of the pendulum and the luscious beauty of these pears will be enjoyed for years to come!

capture the moment

For a gift guaranteed to melt the heart of any mother or grandmother, capture the charm of yesteryear in framed Paper Silhouettes of her precious ones. Turn to page 152 to see how easy it is to craft these old-fashioned portraits from nostalgic family photos. You can even add an extra touch of Victorian wistfulness to the newly created heirlooms by embellishing the frames with ribbon ties. Tears of joy will flow when she opens this box, so be sure to include a box of tissues, too!

etched in time

Encourage a special couple to toast the season by wrapping up a set of holiday goblets for them to share. Embellished with showy snowflakes and soft ribbon bows, these Etched Glasses (page 151) are a romantic gift for newlyweds or a pair who's celebrating their 50th Christmas together.

THE
TASTES
OF
CHRISTMAS

The holiday celebration just wouldn't be complete without the rich aromas and flavors of scrumptious treats from the Christmas kitchen. Keep this impressive collection of recipes close at hand as you prepare the fare for an exceptional Yuletide feast, open house, breakfast, progressive dinner, cookie swap, or other seasonal taste celebration. Many of these specialties can even be made in advance, leaving you more time to visit with family and friends! And for those of you who enjoy sharing from your hearth, we've included a delectable selection of goodies that make great gifts.

Turkey Breast with Cranberry-Nut Stuffing, Sage Gravy

YULETIDE FEAST

Feasting is the key word for this menu extravaganza! Gather family and friends around the table to count your many blessings and to enjoy this traditional Christmas dinner. You'll savor some of your favorite dishes and discover soon-to-be favorites in this tempting fare. Choose an appetizer of soup or salad, or prepare both, and enjoy the good company and conversation as you linger over this holiday spread.

MENU

Butternut Squash Soup • Gourmet Salad Greens • Roasted Onion Dressing • Turkey Breast with Cranberry-Nut Stuffing • Sage Gravy • Orange-Sherry-Glazed Sweet Potatoes • Green Peas with Pine Nuts and Rosemary • Brussels Sprouts Supreme • Sour Cream Dinner Rolls • Company Coconut Cake • Pumpkin Pecan Pie

TURKEY BREAST WITH CRANBERRY-NUT STUFFING

Complete your holiday table with a turkey breast stuffed with seasonal flavors such as cranberries, almonds, and oranges.

- ½ cup chopped onion
- ¼ cup slivered almonds
- ½ cup butter, melted
- 4 cups herbed bread cubes
- 1 cup chopped fresh cranberries
- ½ cup orange juice
- 3 tablespoons sugar
- 2 tablespoons grated orange zest
- 1 bone-in turkey breast (5 pounds)
- ½ teaspoon salt
- ¼ teaspoon ground black pepper
- ¼ cup orange marmalade
- 1 tablespoon butter
- ¼ teaspoon ground ginger
  Fresh herbs, orange slices, and fresh cranberries to garnish

In a large skillet, cook onion and almonds in ½ cup melted butter until onion is tender, stirring often. Stir in bread cubes and next 4 ingredients.

Preheat oven to 325 degrees. Sprinkle turkey cavity with salt and pepper. Tightly pack cavity with 2 cups stuffing. Place remaining stuffing in a greased 1-quart baking dish; cover and chill. Place turkey, skin side up, on a rack in a roasting pan. Bake, uncovered, 1½ hours. Combine marmalade,

1 tablespoon butter, and ginger in a small bowl; brush mixture over turkey breast. Bake turkey 30 more minutes or until a meat thermometer registers 170 degrees, basting every 10 minutes with additional marmalade mixture. Bake reserved stuffing, uncovered, during last 30 minutes of baking time. Garnish platter with fresh herbs, orange slices, and cranberries.
Yield: about 12 servings

SAGE GRAVY

- 2 tablespoons butter
- 2 tablespoons olive oil
- ½ cup finely chopped onion
- ½ cup finely chopped carrot
- ¼ cup finely chopped celery
- 1 tablespoon finely chopped fresh sage leaves OR 1 teaspoon dried sage leaves, crumbled
- ⅓ cup dry white wine
- ½ cup chicken broth
- 1 cup half-and-half
- ½ teaspoon lemon juice
- ½ teaspoon salt
- ½ teaspoon ground black pepper
- 2 tablespoons cold butter, cut into pieces

In a large heavy saucepan, heat butter and olive oil until butter melts. Add onion and next 3 ingredients; cook over medium heat, stirring constantly, until onion is tender. Add wine; bring to a boil and cook until liquid is reduced to about 2 tablespoons.

Add broth and cook until liquid is reduced by half. Stir in half-and-half. Return to a boil; cook until slightly thickened.

Pour mixture through a wire-mesh strainer into a bowl; discard vegetables. Return mixture to saucepan. Stir in lemon juice, salt, and pepper. Add butter pieces, one at a time, stirring with a wire whisk until blended. (If butter is difficult to work into gravy, place saucepan over low heat for a few seconds, being careful not to get mixture too hot.)
Yield: about 2 cups gravy

BUTTERNUT SQUASH SOUP

- 2 medium butternut squash (about 3 pounds)
- 4 cups chicken broth
- 4 cups whipping cream
- ½ cup firmly packed brown sugar
- 1 tablespoon ground cinnamon
- ¼ teaspoon ground nutmeg
  Salt to taste
  Ground white pepper to taste
  Sour cream to garnish

Preheat oven to 350 degrees. Cut each squash in half lengthwise; remove and discard seeds and membranes. Place squash halves, cut side down, in 2 lightly greased 10½ x 15½-inch jellyroll pans. Bake, uncovered, one hour. Let cool to touch; scrape out pulp, discarding rind. Process pulp in a food processor 2 minutes or until smooth.

In a large Dutch oven, combine 4 cups puréed squash (reserve any remaining puréed squash for another use), chicken broth, and next 6 ingredients; stir well. Cook, uncovered, over low heat 10 minutes or until mixture is thoroughly heated, stirring occasionally. Dollop each serving with sour cream.

Yield: about 11 cups soup

SOUR CREAM DINNER ROLLS

- 1 container (8 ounces) sour cream
- ½ cup butter or margarine
- ½ cup sugar
- 1¼ teaspoons salt
- 2 packages dry yeast
- ½ cup warm water (105 degrees to 115 degrees)
- 2 large eggs
- 4 cups all-purpose flour
- 2 tablespoons butter or margarine, melted

In a large saucepan, cook first 4 ingredients over medium-low heat, stirring occasionally, until butter melts. Cool to 105 degrees to 115 degrees.

Combine yeast and ½ cup warm water in a 1-cup glass liquid measuring cup; let stand 5 minutes.

Butternut Squash Soup, Sour Cream Dinner Rolls

In a large bowl, stir together yeast mixture, sour cream mixture, eggs, and flour until well blended. Chill, covered, 8 hours.

Divide dough into fourths; shape each portion into a ball on a lightly floured surface. Use a floured rolling pin to roll each into ¼-inch thickness. Cut dough with a 2½ to 3-inch round cutter. Brush rounds evenly with 2 tablespoons melted butter.

Make a crease across each round with a knife and fold in half, pressing edges to seal. Place rolls, with sides touching, in a greased 10½ x 15½-inch jellyroll pan.

Cover and let rise in a warm place (80 to 85 degrees) 45 minutes or until doubled in size.

Preheat oven to 375 degrees. Bake 12 to 15 minutes or until golden.

Yield: about 4 dozen rolls

GOURMET SALAD GREENS

5½ cups washed, drained, and
    torn assorted salad greens
    (we used butter lettuce, red
    leaf lettuce, and endive)
1½ cups sweet baby broccoli
    flowerets
1 small red onion, cut in half and
    thinly sliced

In a large bowl, lightly toss assorted
salad greens, baby broccoli, and red
onion.
Yield: about 7½ cups salad

ROASTED ONION DRESSING

5 cups chopped onions
2 tablespoons olive oil
1 cup mayonnaise
1 cup buttermilk
½ cup sour cream
2 tablespoons freshly squeezed
    lemon juice
¼ teaspoon dry mustard
¼ teaspoon salt

Preheat oven to 500 degrees.
Combine onions and olive oil on a
10½ x 15½-inch lightly greased
jellyroll pan. Spread in a single layer.
Roast 30 minutes, stirring after every
10 minutes. Let onions cool in pan.

In a medium bowl, combine
mayonnaise, buttermilk, sour cream,
lemon juice, mustard, and salt; stir until
smooth. Stir in onions. Store in an
airtight container in refrigerator. Serve
with green salad.
Yield: about 2¾ cups dressing

Gourmet Salad Greens, Roasted Onion Dressing

Orange-Sherry-Glazed Sweet Potatoes

ORANGE-SHERRY-GLAZED SWEET POTATOES

- 6 medium fresh sweet potatoes
- ¼ teaspoon salt
- ½ cup firmly packed brown sugar
- 1 tablespoon cornstarch
- 1 cup orange juice
- ¼ cup butter or margarine
- 3 tablespoons dry sherry
- ½ cup chopped walnuts

In a medium Dutch oven, cover sweet potatoes with water. Cook over medium-high heat 20 to 25 minutes or until tender. Cool slightly. Peel and quarter sweet potatoes. Arrange in a 9 x 13-inch baking dish. Sprinkle sweet potatoes with salt.

Preheat oven to 350 degrees. In a medium saucepan, combine brown sugar and cornstarch. Stir in orange juice. Cook over medium heat until mixture boils. Stirring constantly, cook about 2 minutes or until mixture thickens. Stir in butter, sherry, and walnuts. Pour over sweet potatoes. Bake, uncovered, 25 to 30 minutes or until bubbly hot.
Yield: about 8 servings

GREEN PEAS WITH PINE NUTS AND ROSEMARY

- ½ cup chicken broth
- 2 packages (10 ounces each) frozen English peas, thawed
- 3 green onions, cut into ½-inch pieces
- ½ teaspoon sugar
- ¾ cup pine nuts
- 3 tablespoons butter or margarine, melted
- 1 tablespoon chopped fresh rosemary
  Salt and ground black pepper to taste
  Fresh rosemary sprigs to garnish

In a medium saucepan, bring chicken broth to a boil over medium-high heat. Add peas, green onions, and sugar; cover, reduce heat, and simmer 5 minutes or until peas are tender. Drain well and set aside.

In a large saucepan, cook pine nuts in butter over medium heat, stirring constantly, 2 to 3 minutes or until golden. Add pea mixture, chopped rosemary, and salt and pepper; cook, uncovered, 2 minutes or until thoroughly heated. Garnish with fresh rosemary.
Yield: about 8 servings

Brussels Sprouts Supreme

Green Peas with Pine Nuts and Rosemary

BRUSSELS SPROUTS SUPREME

This divine flavor festival will make converts out of non-brussels sprouts eaters.

1 pound fresh brussels sprouts
1 teaspoon sugar
1 can (10¾ ounces) cream of chicken soup, undiluted
1 can (8 ounces) sliced water chestnuts, drained
1 cup mayonnaise
2 tablespoons freshly squeezed lemon juice
1 tablespoon freshly grated onion
½ teaspoon ground nutmeg
½ teaspoon dried dill weed
¼ teaspoon salt
¼ teaspoon garlic powder
¼ teaspoon dried tarragon
¼ teaspoon ground black pepper
Dash hot pepper sauce
1½ cups crushed round butter-flavored crackers (about 35 crackers)
⅓ cup grated Parmesan cheese
⅛ teaspoon garlic powder
¼ cup butter or margarine, melted

Wash brussels sprouts; remove discolored leaves. Cut off stem ends and cut a shallow "X" in the bottom of each sprout. In a saucepan, place brussels sprouts and sugar; add water to cover. Bring to a boil; cover, reduce heat, and simmer 8 to 10 minutes or until almost tender. Drain and transfer to a buttered 7 x 11-inch baking dish.

Meanwhile, in a medium bowl, combine soup and next 11 ingredients; stir well. Spoon sauce over sprouts in dish.

Preheat oven to 350 degrees. In a medium bowl, combine cracker crumbs, Parmesan cheese, and ⅛ teaspoon garlic powder; add melted butter, stirring well. Sprinkle over sauce. Bake, uncovered, 20 minutes or until bubbly.

Yield: about 8 servings

COMPANY COCONUT CAKE

If you avoid baking coconut cake because you think it's too involved, then you're in for a pleasant surprise. This version features a cake mix as the main ingredient but tastes like it's made from scratch. We gave it our highest rating.

CAKE

- 3 large eggs
- 1 container (8 ounces) sour cream
- ¾ cup vegetable oil
- ¾ cup cream of coconut
- ½ teaspoon vanilla extract
- 1 package (18¼ ounces) white cake mix with pudding in the mix

COCONUT-CREAM CHEESE FROSTING

- 1 package (8 ounces) cream cheese, softened
- ½ cup butter or margarine, softened
- 1 teaspoon vanilla extract
- 1 package (16 ounces) confectioners sugar
- 1 package (14 ounces) flaked coconut, divided

For cake, preheat oven to 325 degrees. Grease and flour three 8-inch round cake pans. Set pans aside.

Beat eggs at high speed of an electric mixer 2 minutes. Add sour cream and next 3 ingredients, beating well after each addition. Add cake mix; beat at low speed until blended. Beat at high speed 2 minutes. Pour batter into pans. Bake 35 minutes or until a toothpick inserted in center of cake comes out clean. Cool in pans on wire racks 10 minutes; remove from pans and let cool completely on wire racks.

For Coconut-Cream Cheese Frosting, beat cream cheese and butter at medium speed of an electric mixer until creamy; add vanilla, beating well. Gradually add confectioners sugar, beating until smooth. Stir in 2⅔ cups coconut.

Spread frosting between layers and on top and sides of cake. Sprinkle top and sides of cake with remaining coconut. Store in refrigerator in an airtight container.

Yield: about 16 servings

Company Coconut Cake

Pumpkin Pecan Pie with Cinnamon Pastry Crust

PUMPKIN PECAN PIE WITH CINNAMON PASTRY CRUST

CINNAMON PASTRY CRUST
1¼ cups all-purpose flour
½ teaspoon salt
½ teaspoon ground cinnamon
⅓ cup plus 1 tablespoon vegetable shortening
3 to 4 tablespoons ice water

PIE
1 cup sugar
1 cup canned pumpkin
3 large eggs, lightly beaten
½ cup dark corn syrup
1 teaspoon vanilla extract
½ teaspoon ground cinnamon
¼ teaspoon salt
1 cup chopped pecans

For Cinnamon Pastry Crust, combine flour, salt, and cinnamon; cut in shortening with a pastry blender until crumbly. Sprinkle ice water, 1 tablespoon at a time, over surface; stir with a fork until dry ingredients are moistened. Shape into a ball; cover dough and chill until ready to use.

On a lightly floured surface, use a floured rolling pin to roll out dough to ⅛-inch thickness. Transfer to a 9-inch pie plate; use a sharp knife to trim edge of dough. Fold edges under and crimp. Chill 30 minutes.

For pie, preheat oven to 350 degrees. In a large bowl, combine sugar, pumpkin, eggs, corn syrup, vanilla, cinnamon, and salt; stir well with a wire whisk until blended. Pour mixture into crust; sprinkle with pecans.

Bake 50 to 55 minutes or until a knife inserted in center of pie comes out clean. (If edge of crust browns too quickly, cover with a strip of aluminum foil.) Cool completely on a wire rack.

Yield: about 8 servings

75

Marinated Pork Tenderloin Sandwiches, Jezebel Sauce

CHRISTMAS EVE OPEN HOUSE

Open your home to family and friends on the afternoon of Christmas Eve. It's a perfect time to have people drop by for Christmas cheer and a sampling of appetizers as they're out and about delivering presents. Little sandwiches made with Marinated Pork Tenderloin and spread with robust Jezebel Sauce will be the talk of the party. And you'll appreciate the convenience of our Four-Layer Cheese Loaf and Olive Phyllo Shells, which can be made up to a month ahead and frozen. With recipes like these, you'll enjoy the party as much as your guests!

MARINATED PORK TENDERLOIN SANDWICHES

¼ cup lite soy sauce
¼ cup dry sherry or
    Madeira
2 tablespoons olive oil
1 tablespoon dry mustard
1 teaspoon ground ginger
1 teaspoon sesame oil
8 drops hot sauce
2 cloves garlic, minced
2 pork tenderloins (¾ pound
    each)
½ cup apple cider vinegar
3 dozen party rolls
    Jezebel Sauce

In a shallow dish or large heavy-duty resealable plastic bag, combine first 8 ingredients; add tenderloins. Cover or seal and chill 8 hours, turning tenderloins occasionally.

Remove tenderloins from marinade, reserving ½ cup marinade. In a saucepan, combine reserved marinade and apple cider vinegar; bring to a boil and set aside.

Cook tenderloins, covered with grill lid, over medium-hot coals (350 to 400 degrees) 20 to 25 minutes or until a meat thermometer registers 160 degrees, turning occasionally and basting with marinade mixture during first 15 minutes of cooking time. Remove tenderloins from heat; let stand 5 minutes. Slice and serve warm or chilled with party rolls and Jezebel Sauce.

Yield: 36 appetizer sandwiches
Note: Tenderloins may be baked at 400 degrees for 25 minutes instead of grilling, if desired.

JEZEBEL SAUCE

1 cup apple jelly
1 cup pineapple-orange
    marmalade OR pineapple
    preserves
1 jar (6 ounces) prepared
    mustard
1 jar (5 ounces) prepared
    horseradish
¼ teaspoon ground black pepper

In a mixing bowl, beat apple jelly at medium speed of an electric mixer until smooth. Add marmalade and remaining ingredients; beat at medium speed until blended. Cover and chill.
Yield: about 3 cups sauce

Olive Phyllo Shells, Smoked Salmon Spread

SMOKED SALMON SPREAD

12 ounces smoked salmon, divided
2 packages (3 ounces each) cream cheese, softened
¼ cup butter or margarine, softened
1 teaspoon hot pepper sauce
2 teaspoons lemon juice
¼ cup coarsely chopped red onion
  Minced red onion to garnish
  Assorted crackers to serve

Process 9 ounces salmon and next 5 ingredients in a food processor until salmon is coarsely chopped, stopping to scrape down sides. Stir in remaining 3 ounces salmon. Serve immediately or cover and chill 2 hours. Garnish with minced red onion. Serve with assorted crackers.
Yield: about 2 cups salmon spread

OLIVE PHYLLO SHELLS

You can vary the types of nuts and flavors of cheese in these crispy appetizer bites to suit your taste.

1 cup chopped pecans, toasted
1 cup (4 ounces) shredded Cheddar cheese
1 cup chopped pimiento-stuffed olives
2 tablespoons mayonnaise
2 packages (21 ounces each) frozen mini phyllo shells

Stir together first 4 ingredients. Remove phyllo shells from package, leaving them in tray. Spoon 1 teaspoon cheese mixture into each phyllo shell; place tray in a heavy-duty resealable plastic bag and freeze up to one month.

Preheat oven to 375 degrees. Remove phyllo shells from tray and place on a baking sheet. Let stand 10 minutes. Bake cups 12 to 15 minutes or until thoroughly heated. Serve immediately.
Yield: 30 appetizer servings
Note: Olive cups may be baked after assembling at 375 degrees 12 minutes. Serve immediately.

WHITE BEAN DIP

1 can (15.8 ounces) white beans, drained and rinsed
½ cup sour cream
¼ cup Dijon-style mustard
¼ cup chopped fresh parsley
2 tablespoons prepared horseradish
2 tablespoons finely chopped onion
½ teaspoon salt
Fresh parsley sprigs to garnish
Herbed Pita Wedges or tortilla chips to serve

Process white beans, sour cream, mustard, ¼ cup parsley, horseradish, onion, and salt in a food processor until smooth. Garnish with fresh parsley sprigs. Serve with Herbed Pita Wedges or tortilla chips.
Yield: about 2 cups dip

HERBED PITA WEDGES

10 pita bread rounds
½ cup butter or margarine
1½ teaspoons garlic powder
1 teaspoon dried basil leaves
1 teaspoon dried marjoram leaves
1 teaspoon dried thyme leaves
1 teaspoon dried parsley flakes

Cut each pita bread round into quarters, then separate each quarter in half for a total of 80 wedges.
Preheat broiler. Place bread on an ungreased baking sheet. In a small saucepan, melt butter. Stir in garlic powder, basil, marjoram, thyme, and parsley. Remove from heat. Lightly brush butter mixture over both sides of bread. Broil 5½ inches from heat 1½ minutes; turn wedges and broil 30 more seconds. Serve warm.
Yield: 80 pita wedges

White Bean Dip, Herbed Pita Wedges

HERB MARINATED SHRIMP

- 3 quarts water
- 1 large lemon, sliced
- 4 pounds unpeeled large fresh shrimp
- 2 cups vegetable oil
- ¼ cup hot pepper sauce
- 1 tablespoon minced garlic
- 1 tablespoon olive oil
- 1½ teaspoons salt
- 1½ teaspoons seafood seasoning
- 1½ teaspoons dried basil leaves
- 1½ teaspoons dried oregano leaves
- 1½ teaspoons dried thyme leaves
- 1½ teaspoons minced fresh parsley

Bring water and lemon to a boil; add shrimp and cook 3 to 5 minutes or until shrimp turn pink. Drain well; rinse with cold water. Chill. Peel and devein shrimp. Place shrimp in a large heavy-duty resealable plastic bag.

Combine vegetable oil and remaining 9 ingredients; stir well and pour over shrimp. Seal bag; marinate in refrigerator 8 hours. Drain before serving.

Yield: about 25 appetizer servings

FOUR-LAYER CHEESE LOAF

To make two cheese loaves, use two (3 x 7½-inch) loaf pans. Mix ingredients as directed; divide mixtures in half, and follow layering procedure for each loaf.

- 4 cups (16 ounces) shredded sharp Cheddar cheese
- ½ cup chopped pecans, toasted
- ½ cup mayonnaise
- 1 package (10 ounces) frozen chopped spinach, thawed and squeezed dry
- 2 packages (8 ounces each) cream cheese, softened and divided
- ¼ teaspoon salt
- ½ teaspoon ground black pepper
- ¼ cup chutney
- ¼ teaspoon ground nutmeg
  Assorted crackers to serve

Line a 5 x 9-inch loaf pan with heavy-duty plastic wrap.

Combine Cheddar cheese, pecans, and mayonnaise; spread half of mixture

Herb Marinated Shrimp, Four-Layer Cheese Loaf

evenly into prepared pan. Combine spinach, 1 package cream cheese, salt, and pepper; spread evenly over Cheddar cheese layer. Combine remaining package cream cheese, chutney, and nutmeg; spread evenly over spinach layer. Top with remaining Cheddar cheese mixture. Cover and freeze up to one month. Thaw in refrigerator overnight. Serve with assorted crackers.

Yield: about 25 appetizer servings

MINT CHEESECAKE BITES

Here's an easy way to bake and serve cheesecake for a crowd.

- 3 cups chocolate sandwich cookie crumbs (40 cookies)
- ½ cup butter or margarine, melted
- 4 packages (8 ounces) cream cheese, softened
- 1 cup sugar
- 4 large eggs
- 1½ teaspoons peppermint extract
- 6 drops green liquid food coloring
- ½ cup semisweet chocolate chips
- 1 teaspoon vegetable shortening

Preheat oven to 350 degrees. Combine cookie crumbs and butter; press mixture into an aluminum foil-lined 9 x 13-inch baking pan. Bake 10 minutes. Cool on a wire rack.

Beat cream cheese and sugar at medium speed of an electric mixer until creamy. Add eggs, one at a time, beating just until blended after each addition.

Stir in peppermint extract and food coloring. Spread cream cheese mixture over prepared crust.

Reduce heat to 300 degrees. Bake 35 minutes or until set. Cool on a wire rack. Cover and chill 8 hours.

Place chocolate chips and shortening in a small heavy-duty resealable plastic bag; seal. Submerge bag in hot water until chocolate melts; gently knead until mixture is smooth. Snip a tiny hole in one corner of plastic bag; drizzle chocolate over cheesecake. Cut into squares.

Yield: about 24 cheesecake bites

HOT WHITE RUSSIANS

White Russians are usually served over ice. Enjoy this version as a warming after-dinner drink.

- 5 cups freshly brewed coffee
- 1 cup whipping cream
- 1 cup Kahlúa or other coffee-flavored liqueur
- ½ cup vodka
  Whipped cream to garnish

In a large saucepan, combine first 4 ingredients. Cook over medium heat until thoroughly heated.

Warm mugs or cups by rinsing with boiling water. Divide mixture evenly among mugs and top each serving with whipped cream. Serve immediately.

Yield: about 7½ cups coffee

Mint Cheesecake Bites, Hot White Russians

Sausage Breakfast Casserole, Christmas Ambrosia, Mocha Coffee

BREAKFAST WITH SANTA

Of course, Santa's delivery takes precedence, but soon thereafter your family's focus will wander to the pleasing aroma of breakfast. These hearty breakfast recipes are guaranteed to fuel the energy of young and old alike as they enjoy their holiday surprises. And don't worry about spending lots of time in the kitchen; most of these dishes can be made ahead, so all you have to do is heat and eat!

SAUSAGE BREAKFAST CASSEROLE

- 1 pound ground pork sausage OR 2 cups cubed cooked ham
- 10 white sandwich bread slices, cubed (6 cups)
- 2 cups (8 ounces) shredded sharp Cheddar cheese
- 6 large eggs
- 2 cups milk
- 1 teaspoon salt
- 1 teaspoon dry mustard
- ¼ teaspoon Worcestershire sauce

In a large skillet, cook sausage over medium heat, stirring until it crumbles and is no longer pink; drain well.

Place bread cubes in a lightly greased 9 x 13-inch baking dish; sprinkle evenly with cheese and top with sausage.

Whisk together eggs, milk, salt, dry mustard, and Worcestershire sauce; pour over sausage. Cover and chill 8 hours.

Let stand at room temperature 30 minutes.

Preheat oven to 350 degrees. Bake 45 minutes or until set.

Yield: about 8 servings

Note: Casserole may be baked after chilling 1 hour. Omit standing time, and bake as directed.

CHRISTMAS AMBROSIA

- 12 small oranges
- 1 can (20 ounces) pineapple tidbits, drained
- 2 cups flaked coconut
  Maraschino cherries with stems to garnish

Peel and section oranges, catching juice in a large nonmetal bowl. Add orange sections, pineapple, and coconut to juice; toss gently. Cover and chill thoroughly.

To serve, spoon fruit mixture into a large serving bowl or individual dishes. Garnish with maraschino cherries.

Yield: 6 to 8 servings

MOCHA COFFEE

- ¾ cup ground coffee
- 4 cinnamon sticks (each 3 inches)
- 1½ teaspoons whole cloves
- 8 cups water
- ¼ cup chocolate syrup
- ½ cup sugar
- ½ teaspoon anise extract
  Whipped cream and candy canes to garnish

In a coffee filter or filter basket, place ground coffee, cinnamon sticks, and cloves. Add water to coffeemaker, and brew.

Stir syrup, sugar, and anise into brewed coffee. Pour into mugs; dollop each serving with whipped cream. Garnish with a candy cane.

Yield: about 8 cups coffee

SAUSAGE BISCUITS

½ pound ground pork sausage
⅓ cup vegetable shortening
2 cups self-rising flour
⅔ cup buttermilk

In a large skillet, cook sausage over medium-high heat, stirring until it crumbles and is no longer pink. Drain well and set aside.

With a pastry blender, cut shortening into flour until crumbly; add buttermilk, stirring until dry ingredients are moistened. Add sausage; gently knead into dough.

Preheat oven to 450 degrees. On a lightly foured surface, use a floured rolling pin to roll out dough to ¼-inch thickness; cut with a 2½-inch round cutter. Place on lightly greased baking sheets. Bake 11 minutes or until lightly browned.

Yield: about 12 biscuits

GARLIC-CHEESE GRITS

7 cups water
2 teaspoons salt
2 cups uncooked quick-cooking grits
3 cloves garlic, minced
1 container (16 ounces) pasteurized process cheese, cubed
½ cup half-and-half
⅓ cup butter or margarine
Ground red pepper or paprika to garnish

In a Dutch oven, bring water and salt to a boil; gradually stir in grits and garlic. Cover, reduce heat, and simmer 5 minutes, stirring occasionally.

Add cheese, half-and-half, and butter; simmer, stirring constantly, until cheese and butter melt. Sprinkle ground red pepper on top to garnish.

Yield: about 15 servings

Sausage Biscuits, Garlic-Cheese Grits

Ham and Eggs Burritos, Mexican Marys

HAM AND EGGS BURRITOS

⅔ cup butter or margarine, divided
12 eggs
3 tablespoons water
¾ teaspoon salt
¼ teaspoon ground black pepper
1½ cups chopped ham
2 packages (8.5 ounces each) flour tortillas (about 7-inch diameter)
12 ounces Monterey Jack Cheese with jalapeño peppers, thinly sliced
Fresh cilantro to garnish
Salsa and sour cream to serve

In a large skillet, melt ⅓ cup butter over medium-low heat. In a small bowl, beat eggs, water, salt, and black pepper until well blended. Stirring occasionally, cook egg mixture in butter until eggs are set. Stir in ham. Cover and remove from heat.

Preheat oven to 325 degrees. In a small saucepan, melt remaining ⅓ cup butter. Brush one side of each tortilla with melted butter. Place a slice of cheese on one buttered edge of each tortilla. Spoon about 3 tablespoons egg mixture over cheese slice. Beginning with this edge, roll up tortilla. Place burritos in a lightly greased 9 x 13-inch baking dish. Cover with aluminum foil. Bake covered burritos in oven about 30 minutes or until cheese melts. Garnish with fresh cilantro. Serve warm with salsa and sour cream.

Yield: about 20 burritos

MEXICAN MARYS

4½ cups tomato juice, chilled
¼ cup lime juice
3 tablespoons Worcestershire sauce
1 tablespoon prepared horseradish
1 teaspoon celery salt
½ teaspoon ground black pepper
¼ to ½ teaspoon jalapeño pepper sauce
¼ teaspoon ground cumin
1 cup vodka
Celery ribs to garnish

Combine first 8 ingredients; stir well and chill. Stir in vodka and serve over ice. Garnish with celery ribs.

Yield: about 6 cups beverage

CRANBERRY STREUSEL MUFFINS

1¾ cups all-purpose flour
½ cup sugar
2¾ teaspoons baking powder
2 teaspoons grated lemon zest
¾ teaspoon salt
1 large egg, lightly beaten
¾ cup milk
⅓ cup vegetable oil
1 cup sweetened dried cranberries
1 tablespoon all-purpose flour
1 tablespoon sugar
¼ cup sugar
2½ tablespoons all-purpose flour
½ teaspoon ground cinnamon
1½ tablespoons butter or
    margarine

Preheat oven to 400 degrees. In a large bowl, combine first 5 ingredients; make a well in center of mixture. Combine egg, milk, and oil; stir well. Add to dry ingredients, stirring just until moistened.

Combine cranberries, 1 tablespoon flour, and 1 tablespoon sugar, tossing gently to coat. Fold cranberry mixture into batter. Fill greased muffin cups about two-thirds full.

Combine ¼ cup sugar, 2½ tablespoons flour, and cinnamon; with a pastry blender, cut in butter until crumbly. Sprinkle over batter. Bake 18 minutes or until tops are golden. Remove from pans immediately.
Yield: about 10 muffins

CHERRY-CREAM CHEESE COFFEE CAKE

½ package (32 ounces) frozen
    bread dough, thawed
½ cup cream cheese, softened
2 tablespoons granulated sugar,
    divided
1 teaspoon vanilla extract
⅓ cup dried cherries
1½ tablespoons honey
1 tablespoon milk
½ cup confectioners sugar
2½ teaspoons milk
¼ teaspoon vanilla extract

Preheat oven to 375 degrees. Roll dough into an 8 x 12-inch rectangle on a lightly greased baking sheet.

Cranberry Streusel Muffins, Cherry-Cream Cheese Coffee Cake

Combine cream cheese, 1 tablespoon granulated sugar, and 1 teaspoon vanilla, stirring well. Spoon cheese mixture lengthwise down center third of dough. Sprinkle cherries over cheese mixture; drizzle with honey.

Along 12-inch sides of rectangle, cut 12 (1-inch-wide) strips from edge of filling to edge of dough. Fold strips, alternating sides, at an angle across filling, tucking in strips securely. Brush

top of dough with 1 tablespoon milk. Sprinkle with remaining 1 tablespoon granulated sugar. Bake 20 minutes or until golden.

Combine confectioners sugar, 2½ teaspoons milk, and ¼ teaspoon vanilla, stirring well. Drizzle sugar mixture over warm coffee cake.
Yield: 1 loaf coffee cake

APRICOT-CHEESE CRESCENTS

- 2 cups all-purpose flour
- ½ teaspoon salt
- 1 cup butter, cut up
- 1 container (12 ounces) small-curd cottage cheese
- 1 package (6 ounces) dried apricots
- ½ cup water
- 1 cup sugar, divided
- 1 egg white, lightly beaten
- ¾ cup finely chopped almonds

Combine flour and salt. With a pastry blender, cut in butter until crumbly. Stir in cottage cheese until blended. Shape mixture into 1½-inch balls. Cover and chill 8 hours.

In a saucepan, bring apricots and ½ cup water to a boil; cover, reduce heat, and simmer 15 minutes. Remove from heat; cool 10 minutes.

Process apricot mixture and ½ cup sugar in a food processor until smooth, stopping to scrape sides.

Preheat oven to 375 degrees. On a lightly floured surface, pat each ball into a 3-inch-diameter circle. Spoon 1 teaspoon apricot mixture in center of each circle. Fold circles in half, pressing edges to seal.

Place on lightly greased baking sheets. Brush with egg white. Stir together remaining ½ cup sugar and almonds; sprinkle evenly over crescents. Bake 18 to 20 minutes or until lightly browned.

Yield: about 3½ dozen crescents

RUSSIAN TEA

- 2 cups sugar
- 2 cups orange-flavored powdered instant breakfast drink
- ⅔ cup presweetened lemonade mix
- ½ cup instant tea mix
- 1 tablespoon ground cinnamon
- 1 tablespoon ground cloves
  Cinnamon sticks to garnish

Combine all ingredients. Store in an airtight container.

To serve, place 2 heaping tablespoons mix in a cup or mug. Add ¾ cup boiling water; stir well. Garnish with cinnamon sticks.

Yield: about 4½ cups mix or about 36 (6-ounce) servings

Apricot-Cheese Crescents, Russian Tea

Party Meatballs, Fruited Cheddar Ball, Mexi Spiced Nuts

NEIGHBOR TO NEIGHBOR

A progressive dinner is a unique way for neighborhood friends or supper clubs to entertain during the holidays — plus the cooking can be divided up among several people! Serve these recipes for a successful and festive evening, and plan on three stops — appetizers, main course, and dessert. Let the party begin!

PARTY MEATBALLS

- 1 small onion, quartered
- 1/3 cup water
- 1 large egg
- 1 tablespoon sugar
- 1 1/4 teaspoons salt
- 1 teaspoon dried marjoram leaves
- 1/2 teaspoon curry powder
- 1/4 teaspoon dried thyme leaves
- 1/4 teaspoon ground ginger
- 1/4 teaspoon ground cloves
- 1/4 teaspoon rubbed sage
- Pinch of ground cinnamon
- Pinch of ground nutmeg
- 1 pound ground beef
- 3/4 cup herb-seasoned stuffing mix
- 2 tablespoons all-purpose flour
- 1 tablespoon vegetable oil
- 1/2 cup prepared mustard
- 1/2 cup ketchup
- 1/2 cup molasses

Process first 13 ingredients in a large food processor until blended. Add beef, stuffing mix, and flour; pulse until blended. Shape beef mixture into 32 balls.

In a large skillet, cook meatballs in 2 batches in hot oil over medium-high heat 7 minutes or until done. (Gently shake pan over burner often to turn and brown meatballs evenly.) Transfer meatballs to a chafing dish or electric slow cooker and keep warm.

In a small saucepan, combine mustard, ketchup, and molasses. Cook over medium heat until sauce is warm. Pour sauce over meatballs and serve warm.

Yield: 32 appetizer meatballs

FRUITED CHEDDAR BALL

This cheese ball is the perfect size for a large gathering, but the mixture can be divided easily into two balls. Freeze one for later, or give one as a gift.

- 3/4 cup dried apricot halves
- 1/3 cup pitted whole dates
- 1/3 cup golden raisins
- 1/4 cup cognac or brandy
- 1 1/2 pounds mild Cheddar cheese, cut into 3/4-inch cubes
- 12 ounces cream cheese, softened
- 1 1/4 cups sliced almonds, toasted and divided
- Assorted crackers and fresh apple slices to serve

Process apricots and dates in a food processor until chopped. Combine chopped fruit, raisins, and cognac in a small bowl; cover and let stand one hour or until liquid is almost absorbed.

Process Cheddar cheese cubes in food processor until finely chopped. Add cream cheese, a third at a time; process just until blended, stopping as needed to scrape down sides. Add fruit mixture and 3/4 cup almonds; pulse 3 times or just until fruit and almonds are chopped and mixture is combined. (Do not overprocess; mixture should be chunky.)

Shape cheese mixture into a ball. Lightly press remaining almonds into cheese ball. Wrap tightly with plastic wrap and chill until firm. Let come to room temperature before serving. Serve with assorted crackers and fresh apple slices.

Yield: one 7-inch cheese ball

MEXI SPICED NUTS

You'll feast on the feisty chili-style flavors of this addictive nut mix.

- 2 cups pecan halves
- 2 cups salted roasted peanuts
- 1 egg white, lightly beaten
- 1/4 cup butter or margarine, melted
- 1 tablespoon chili powder
- 1 teaspoon ground red pepper
- 1/2 teaspoon garlic powder
- 1 tablespoon Worcestershire sauce
- 1 teaspoon hot pepper sauce

Preheat oven to 350 degrees. Combine pecans and peanuts in an ungreased 9 x 13-inch pan.

In a small bowl, combine egg white and remaining ingredients, stirring well; pour over nuts, stirring to coat.

Bake, uncovered, 30 minutes or until toasted; cool completely in pan on a wire rack. Store in an airtight container.

Yield: 4 cups nuts

Tawny Baked Ham, Green Beans with Caramelized Onions

TAWNY BAKED HAM

1 smoked, fully cooked whole
    ham (19 pounds)
⅓ cup Dijon-style mustard
35 whole cloves (about
      2 teaspoons)
1 cup firmly packed brown sugar
2 cups apple juice
2 cups pitted whole dates
2 cups dried figs
2 cups pitted prunes
2 cups tawny port wine

Preheat oven to 350 degrees.
Discard skin from ham. Score fat on
ham in a diamond design. Spread
mustard over top and sides of ham
and insert a clove into each diamond.
Coat ham with brown sugar, pressing
into mustard, if necessary. Place ham,
fat side up, in a lightly greased large
shallow roasting pan. Insert meat
thermometer, making sure it does not
touch fat or bone. Pour apple juice
into pan. Bake, uncovered, 2 hours,
basting often with apple juice.

Combine dates, dried figs, prunes,
and port wine; pour into pan with
ham. Bake ham 30 more minutes or
until meat thermometer registers
140 degrees, basting often with
mixture in pan. Transfer ham to
a serving platter and let stand
10 minutes before slicing. Arrange
fruit mixture around ham. Serve
with pan drippings.
Yield: 35 servings

GREEN BEANS WITH CARAMELIZED ONIONS

3 pounds fresh green beans
3 large sweet onions, cut in half
    and thinly sliced
⅓ cup butter or margarine
⅓ cup firmly packed brown sugar

Cook green beans in boiling water
to cover 15 minutes; drain and chill
overnight, if desired.

In a Dutch oven, cook onion over
medium heat 15 to 20 minutes or
until golden brown, stirring often.
Reduce heat to medium; stir in butter
and brown sugar. Add green beans;
cook 5 minutes or until thoroughly
heated.
Yield: about 12 servings

GREEK RICE SALAD

4 cups cooked long-grain rice
1 can (15.8 ounces) great
    Northern beans, drained and
    rinsed
1 cup (4 ounces) crumbled feta
    cheese
½ cup sliced green onions
½ cup chopped sweet yellow
    pepper
½ cup chopped sweet red pepper
¼ cup chopped fresh parsley
1 can (2¼ ounces) sliced ripe
    olives, drained
2 tablespoons capers, drained
3 tablespoons white balsamic
    vinegar
2 tablespoons olive oil
1 tablespoon Dijon-style mustard
1 clove garlic, minced
1 teaspoon Greek seasoning
½ teaspoon salt
¼ teaspoon ground black pepper

In a large bowl, combine first
9 ingredients. In a small bowl, combine
vinegar, oil, mustard, garlic, Greek
seasoning, salt, and black pepper. Stir
until well blended. Pour over rice

mixture. Stir until well coated. Cover and chill. Store in an airtight container in refrigerator. Serve at room temperature.

Yield: 12 to 15 servings

PEPPERCORN BEEF TENDERLOIN

Colorful peppercorns encrust this beef tenderloin with spicy crunch.

- 1 container (8 ounces) sour cream
- 2 tablespoons prepared horseradish
- 3 tablespoons Dijon-style mustard
- 1 tablespoon red peppercorns
- 1 tablespoon green peppercorns
- 2 teaspoons coarse salt
- 1 cup chopped fresh parsley
- ¼ cup butter, softened
- 3 tablespoons Dijon-style mustard
- 1 beef tenderloin (3 pounds), trimmed
  Fresh rosemary sprigs to garnish

In a small bowl, combine first 3 ingredients; cover and chill.

Place peppercorns in blender; cover and pulse until coarsely chopped. Transfer to a bowl and stir in salt.

Combine parsley, butter, and 3 tablespoons mustard; rub mixture evenly over tenderloin. Roll tenderloin in peppercorn mixture, coating thoroughly. Cover and chill up to 24 hours.

Preheat oven to 450 degrees. Place tenderloin on a lightly greased rack in a shallow roasting pan. Bake 50 minutes or until meat thermometer inserted in thickest portion of tenderloin registers 145 degrees (medium rare) to 160 degrees (medium). Transfer tenderloin to a platter and cover loosely with aluminum foil. Let stand 10 minutes before slicing. Slice and serve with sour cream mixture. Garnish platter with fresh rosemary sprigs.

Yield: about 10 servings

Greek Rice Salad, Peppercorn Beef Tenderloin

ORANGE LIQUEUR CAKE

- 1 package (18¼ ounces) yellow cake mix with pudding in the mix
- 3 large eggs
- 1 tablespoon grated orange rind
- 1 cup freshly squeezed orange juice
- ⅓ cup vegetable oil
- ⅓ cup sour cream
- 1 tablespoon freshly squeezed lemon juice
- 1 tablespoon Cointreau or other orange-flavored liqueur
- ⅓ cup firmly packed brown sugar
- ⅓ cup freshly squeezed orange juice
- 2 tablespoons butter or margarine
- ⅓ cup Cointreau or other orange-flavored liqueur
- ½ cup apricot preserves
- 2 tablespoons orange marmalade
  Orange zest curls and wedges to garnish

Preheat oven to 350 degrees. In a large mixing bowl, combine first 8 ingredients; beat at low speed of an electric mixer 2 minutes. Pour batter into a greased 10-inch fluted tube pan. Bake 35 to 40 minutes or until a toothpick inserted in center of cake comes out clean. Transfer cake in pan to a wire rack.

While cake bakes, combine brown sugar, ⅓ cup orange juice, and butter in a saucepan. Cook over medium heat until sugar dissolves and butter melts, stirring occasionally. Remove from heat; stir in ⅓ cup Cointreau.

Prick warm cake to bottom of pan at 1-inch intervals with a long wooden skewer or cake tester. Spoon warm juice mixture over warm cake. Cool at least 3 hours in pan on a wire rack.

In a small saucepan, combine apricot preserves and orange marmalade. Cook over medium heat, stirring constantly, just until preserves and marmalade melt. Pour mixture through a wire-mesh strainer into a bowl, discarding solids.

Invert cake onto a serving plate. Brush preserve mixture evenly over cake. Garnish with orange zest curls and wedges.
Yield: about 16 servings

COFFEE TART

- ½ cup slivered almonds, toasted
- 20 chocolate wafer cookies
- 1 cup sugar, divided
- ⅓ cup butter or margarine, melted
- ½ cup butter or margarine
- 3 bittersweet chocolate candy bars (4 ounces each), coarsely chopped
- 2 tablespoons instant coffee granules
- 2 cups whipping cream, divided
- 6 egg yolks
  Whipped cream and chocolate-covered coffee beans to garnish

Orange Liqueur Cake

Coffee Tart, Hot Buttered Bourbon

Preheat oven to 350 degrees. Process almonds, cookies, and ¼ cup sugar in a food processor until ground; add ⅓ cup melted butter and pulse to blend. Press into a 10-inch tart pan with a removable bottom. Bake 10 minutes. Cool completely in pan on a wire rack.

In a heavy saucepan, melt ½ cup butter and chocolate over low heat, stirring constantly. Add remaining ¾ cup sugar, coffee granules, and ½ cup whipping cream; cook until sugar dissolves, stirring constantly.

Beat egg yolks until thick and pale. Gradually stir about one-fourth hot chocolate mixture into yolks; add to remaining hot mixture, stirring constantly. Cook over medium heat, stirring constantly, 1 to 2 minutes or until mixture reaches 160 degrees. Remove from heat.

Spread two-thirds chocolate mixture into crust. Cool remaining chocolate mixture 30 minutes.

Beat remaining 1½ cups whipping cream at high speed of an electric mixer until soft peaks form. Stir one-third of whipped cream into remaining chocolate mixture until smooth. Fold in remaining whipped cream. Spread over chocolate layer. Cover and chill at least 2 hours. Garnish with whipped cream and coffee beans.
Yield: about 12 servings

HOT BUTTERED BOURBON

This is almost as good without the bourbon as it is with it.

    1 pound butter, softened
    1 package (16 ounces) light
         brown sugar
    1 package (16 ounces)
         confectioners sugar
    2 teaspoons ground cinnamon
    2 teaspoons ground nutmeg
    1 quart vanilla ice cream,
         softened
    1 liter bourbon
    4 quarts hot brewed coffee
         Sweetened whipped cream and
         ground cinnamon to garnish

In a large bowl, beat butter, brown sugar, confectioners sugar, cinnamon, and nutmeg at medium speed of an electric mixer until light and fluffy. Stir in ice cream; freeze in an airtight container until firm.

In a large bowl, combine ice-cream mixture, bourbon, and hot coffee, stirring well. Or for one serving, combine 3 tablespoons ice-cream mixture, 3 tablespoons bourbon, and ¾ cup coffee in a large mug, stirring well. Dollop each serving with sweetened whipped cream and sprinkle with cinnamon.
Yield: about 20 servings
Note: Ice-cream mixture may be frozen up to one month.

Pumpkin Cheesecake

SWEET FINALES

Let them eat cake . . . and pies, pastries, and all sorts of decadent treats by hosting a dessert party. Most of these luscious desserts can be made ahead so you can spend time enjoying a late evening of merrymaking with your guests. They'll go home satisfied with visions of sugarplums dancing in their heads!

PUMPKIN CHEESECAKE

CHEESECAKE
- ¾ cup granulated sugar, divided
- ¾ cup firmly packed brown sugar, divided
- ¾ cup graham cracker crumbs
- ½ cup finely chopped pecans
- ¼ cup butter or margarine, melted
- 1 tablespoon all-purpose flour
- 1½ teaspoons ground cinnamon
- ½ teaspoon ground ginger
- ½ teaspoon ground nutmeg
- 1 teaspoon vanilla extract
- ¼ teaspoon salt
- 1 can (16 ounces) pumpkin
- 3 packages (8 ounces each) cream cheese, softened
- 3 large eggs

GINGER CREAM TOPPING
- 1 cup whipping cream
- 1 container (8 ounces) sour cream
- 2 tablespoons granulated sugar
- ¼ cup minced crystallized ginger
- 3 tablespoons dark rum
- ½ teaspoon vanilla extract

PECAN CRUNCH
- 2 tablespoons butter or margarine, melted
- 1 cup chopped pecans
- ½ cup granulated sugar

For cheesecake, combine ¼ cup granulated sugar, ¼ cup brown sugar, graham cracker crumbs, ½ cup pecans, and butter; press in bottom and one inch up sides of a lightly greased 9-inch springform pan. Cover and chill one hour.

Preheat oven to 350 degrees. Combine remaining ½ cup sugar, remaining ½ cup brown sugar, flour, and next 6 ingredients; set aside.

In a mixing bowl, beat cream cheese at medium speed of an electric mixer until creamy. Add pumpkin mixture, beating well. Add eggs, one at a time, beating after each addition. Pour mixture into prepared crust. Bake one hour and 15 minutes. Cool completely in pan on a wire rack.

For Ginger Cream Topping, combine whipping cream, sour cream, and granulated sugar in a medium mixing bowl; beat at high speed of an electric mixer until soft peaks form. Fold in ginger, rum, and vanilla. Spoon Ginger Cream Topping over cheesecake. Cover and chill at least 8 hours.

For Pecan Crunch, combine all ingredients in an 8-inch cast-iron skillet; cook over medium heat, stirring constantly, 12 to 14 minutes or until sugar is golden. Pour mixture onto a greased baking sheet. Let mixture cool completely and break into small pieces.

To serve, carefully remove sides of springform pan; sprinkle Pecan Crunch over top of cheesecake.

Yield: 16 servings

Coffee Bar

Instead of serving plain coffee, set up a coffee bar near the dessert table. Brew the coffee with slivered almonds or strips of orange zest for added flavor. Set out brandy or several liqueurs such as kirsch, Galliano, Kahlúa, Triple Sec, Tía Maria, and amaretto to stir into the coffee. Offer sugar cubes, whipped cream, and grated chocolate, and serve with cinnamon stick stirrers. Add maraschino cherries or strawberries to garnish a cloud of whipped cream on top.

TRIPLE CHOCOLATE CAKE

Devil's food cake mix and chocolate pudding mix add to the convenience of this rich, moist cake. The final chocolate in the trio? A full 2 cups of chips that melt throughout the cake as it bakes.

 1 package (18¼ ounces) devil's food cake mix (we used Duncan Hines)
 1 package (12 ounces) semisweet chocolate chips
 1 container (8 ounces) sour cream
 4 large eggs
 ½ cup chopped pecans
 ½ cup water
 ½ cup vegetable oil
 1 package (3.9 ounces) chocolate instant pudding mix
   Confectioners sugar

Preheat oven to 350 degrees. In a large bowl, combine first 8 ingredients; stir with a wire whisk until ingredients are blended. Pour batter into a well-greased 12-cup fluted tube pan.

Bake one hour or until cake begins to pull away from sides of pan. Cool in pan on a wire rack 15 minutes; remove cake from pan and cool completely on wire rack. Sift a small amount of confectioners sugar over cake.
Yield: about 16 servings

TIRAMISU

 2 packages (3.4 ounces each) vanilla instant pudding mix
 4 cups milk
 2 cups mascarpone cheese, softened
 1 container (12 ounces) frozen nondairy whipped topping, thawed and divided
 1 teaspoon instant espresso powder
 ¼ cup hot water
 ¼ cup coffee-flavored liqueur
 3 packages (3 ounces each) ladyfingers (about 36 small ladyfingers)
   Sifted cocoa to garnish

In a medium bowl, combine pudding mix and milk according to package directions. Beat mascarpone cheese

Triple Chocolate Cake, Tiramisu

into chilled pudding. Fold in 3 cups nondairy whipped topping. In a small bowl, dissolve espresso powder in hot water. Stir in liqueur. Line sides and bottom of a 3-quart serving dish with ladyfingers. Brush ⅔ of espresso mixture over ladyfingers. Spoon half of filling into dish. Place remaining ladyfingers on top of filling. Brush remaining espresso mixture over ladyfingers. Cover with remaining filling. Cover and chill.

To serve, spread remaining whipped topping over top of dessert. Sift cocoa on top to garnish.
Yield: 10 to 12 servings

Honey-Crunch Pecan Pie, Raspberry-Almond Tarts

RASPBERRY-ALMOND TARTS

½ cup butter or margarine, softened
1 package (3 ounces) cream cheese, softened
1 cup all-purpose flour
⅓ cup seedless raspberry jam
1 large egg
½ cup sugar
⅓ cup almond paste, crumbled
½ cup whole blanched almonds, coarsely chopped

In a mixing bowl, beat butter and cream cheese at medium speed of an electric mixer until creamy. Add flour and beat until blended. Cover and chill one hour.

Preheat oven to 325 degrees. Shape pastry into 24 (1-inch) balls. Press balls into bottom and up sides of each ungreased cup of a miniature muffin pan. Spoon ½ teaspoon raspberry jam into each tart. Stir together egg, sugar, and almond paste; spoon one teaspoon mixture over jam and sprinkle with chopped almonds. Bake 30 to 35 minutes. Cool slightly in pans on a wire rack; remove from pans and cool completely. Freeze up to one month, if desired.
Yield: 2 dozen tarts

HONEY-CRUNCH PECAN PIE

4 large eggs, lightly beaten
1 cup light corn syrup
¼ cup granulated sugar
¼ cup firmly packed brown sugar
2 tablespoons butter or margarine, melted
1 tablespoon bourbon
1 teaspoon vanilla extract
½ teaspoon salt
1 cup chopped pecans
1 unbaked 10-inch pie crust
¼ cup plus 3 tablespoons firmly packed brown sugar
¼ cup butter or margarine
⅓ cup honey
2 cups pecan halves

Preheat oven to 350 degrees. In a large bowl, combine first 8 ingredients; stir well with a wire whisk until blended. Stir in chopped pecans. Spoon pecan mixture into crust. Bake 35 minutes. (If edge of crust browns too quickly, cover with a strip of aluminum foil.)

Meanwhile, in a medium saucepan, combine ¼ cup plus 3 tablespoons brown sugar, ¼ cup butter, and honey; cook mixture over medium heat 2 minutes or until sugar dissolves and butter melts, stirring mixture often. Add pecan halves and stir gently until pecan halves are coated. Spoon pecan mixture evenly over pie. Bake 12 more minutes or until topping is bubbly. Let cool completely on a wire rack.
Yield: about 8 servings

97

Marshmallow Creme Eggnog, Japanese Fruitcake

JAPANESE FRUITCAKE

A pearly white frosting thinly veils this luscious cake.

CAKE

- 1 cup butter or margarine, softened
- 2 cups sugar
- 4 large eggs
- 3¼ cups all-purpose flour
- 2 teaspoons baking powder
- 1 cup milk
- 1 teaspoon vanilla extract
- 1 teaspoon ground cinnamon
- 1 teaspoon ground allspice
- ½ teaspoon ground cloves
- 1 cup raisins
  Lemon slice to garnish

LEMON-COCONUT FROSTING

- 2 tablespoons cornstarch
- 1½ cups water, divided
- 2 cups sugar
- 1 tablespoon grated lemon zest
- 3½ tablespoons freshly squeezed lemon juice
- 3½ cups frozen flaked coconut, thawed

For cake, preheat oven to 350 degrees. In a mixing bowl, beat butter at medium speed of an electric mixer until creamy. Gradually add sugar, beating well. Add eggs, one at a time, beating well after each addition.

Combine flour and baking powder. Mixing at low speed, add dry ingredients to butter mixture alternately with milk, beginning and ending with flour mixture. Add vanilla, stirring to blend. Pour one-third of batter into a greased and floured 9-inch round cake pan.

Stir cinnamon, allspice, cloves, and raisins into remaining batter; pour mixture into 2 greased and floured 9-inch round cake pans.

Bake 25 minutes or until center of cake springs back when lightly touched. (Do not overbake.) Cool in pans on wire racks 10 minutes; remove from pans and cool completely on wire racks.

For Lemon-Coconut Frosting, combine cornstarch and ½ cup water, stirring until smooth; set aside.

In a medium saucepan, bring remaining 1 cup water to a boil. Stir in

MARSHMALLOW CREME EGGNOG

Here's an extravagant take on a classic holiday indulgence.

- 4 cups milk
- ½ cup marshmallow creme
- 3 tablespoons sugar
- ½ vanilla bean, split lengthwise
- 1⅔ cups egg substitute
- ½ cup bourbon (optional)
- ½ teaspoon freshly grated nutmeg (optional)
- 2 cups vanilla ice cream, softened
  Freshly grated nutmeg to garnish

In a large saucepan, combine milk, marshmallow creme, sugar, and vanilla bean; cook over medium-low heat until marshmallow creme melts, stirring often.

Pour egg substitute into a bowl. Gradually stir about one-fourth of hot mixture into egg substitute; add to remaining hot mixture, stirring constantly. Cook over medium-low heat, stirring constantly, 3 to 4 minutes or until thickened; remove from heat. If desired, stir in bourbon and ½ teaspoon nutmeg. Let stand until cool. Cover and chill 3 hours; remove and discard vanilla bean.

Stir in ice cream just before serving. Garnish with freshly grated nutmeg.

Yield: 8 cups eggnog

Mocha Toffee, Peppermint Christmas Cookies

2 cups sugar, lemon zest, and lemon juice. Return to a boil and cook until mixture reaches soft ball stage (236 degrees), stirring often.

Gradually stir in cornstarch mixture; cook, stirring constantly, over medium heat about 10 minutes or until thickened. Remove from heat; stir in coconut. Cool. Stir frosting just before spreading on cake. Spread frosting between layers and on top and sides of cake, stacking white layer between spiced layers. Garnish with a slice of lemon.

Yield: about 16 servings

MOCHA TOFFEE

1	tablespoon instant coffee granules
1/3	cup hot water
1	cup butter
1	cup sugar
1	tablespoon light corn syrup
2	cups slivered almonds, toasted and coarsely ground
1	teaspoon vanilla extract
1/2	cup semisweet chocolate mini chips

Line a baking sheet with aluminum foil, extending foil over ends of pan; grease foil. Butter sides of a very heavy large saucepan.

In a small bowl, dissolve coffee granules in hot water. In heavy saucepan, combine butter, sugar, corn syrup, and coffee. Stirring constantly, cook over medium-low heat until sugar dissolves. Using a pastry brush dipped in hot water, wash down any sugar crystals on sides of pan. Attach a candy thermometer to pan. Stirring constantly, bring to a boil over medium heat. Cook, without stirring, until mixture reaches hard-crack stage (approximately 300 to 310 degrees). Remove from heat and stir in almonds and vanilla.

Spread mixture onto prepared baking sheet. Sprinkle chocolate chips over hot toffee; spread melted chocolate over toffee. Chill one hour or until chocolate hardens. Break into pieces. Store in an airtight container in a cool place.

Yield: about 1½ pounds toffee

PEPPERMINT CHRISTMAS COOKIES

3/4	cup butter or margarine, softened
1/2	cup sugar, divided
1	egg yolk
1	teaspoon vanilla extract
1 3/4	cups all-purpose flour
1/3	cup crushed hard peppermint candy
1	package (8 ounces) milk chocolate candies

Preheat oven to 350 degrees. In a large mixing bowl, beat butter at medium speed of an electric mixer until creamy; gradually add ¼ cup sugar, beating well. Add egg yolk and vanilla, beating well. Gradually add flour and crushed peppermint, beating well. Shape dough into 1-inch balls. Roll balls in remaining ¼ cup sugar; place 2 inches apart on lightly greased baking sheets.

Bake 5 minutes. Immediately press a chocolate candy into center of each cookie; bake 6 minutes. Cool cookies one minute on baking sheets; transfer to wire racks to cool completely.

Yield: about 3 dozen cookies

Christmas Cookie Cutouts, Shining Star Shortbread

SWAPPING SWEETS

Host a cookie swap to exchange sweet confections with your friends during the holidays. Have each guest make a dozen cookies for each person who will be attending plus extras for nibbling at the party. Your family will love the variety that you return home with, and you will, too, because you have to bake only once! Remember to bring copies of the recipes to share.

CHRISTMAS COOKIE CUTOUTS

COOKIES
2 cups butter or margarine, softened
1 cup granulated sugar
3 egg yolks
4 cups all-purpose flour
1/4 teaspoon baking powder
1/4 teaspoon salt
2 teaspoons vanilla extract
1 teaspoon almond extract

CONFECTIONERS SUGAR PAINTS
3 cups confectioners sugar
2 tablespoons light corn syrup
1 teaspoon vanilla extract
2 to 3 tablespoons milk
Assorted liquid food coloring

For cookies, beat butter at medium speed of an electric mixer until creamy; gradually add granulated sugar, beating well. Add egg yolks, one at a time, beating until blended after each addition.

Combine flour, baking powder, and salt; gradually add to butter mixture, beating at low speed after each addition. Stir in extracts. Divide dough in half; wrap each half in plastic wrap. Chill at least 4 hours.

Preheat oven to 350 degrees. On a lightly floured surface, use a floured

rolling pin to roll out half of dough to 1/4-inch thickness. Cut with 3-inch cookie cutters and place 2 inches apart on lightly greased baking sheets. Bake 15 minutes or until edges are golden. Cool cookies on baking sheets on wire racks 3 minutes; transfer to wire racks to cool completely. Repeat with remaining dough.

For Confectioners Sugar Paints, stir together confectioners sugar and corn syrup; stir in vanilla and enough milk to make desired spreading or piping consistency. Divide into several small bowls; stir drops of a different food coloring into each. Decorate cookies with colored paints or icing, using a small spatula or paintbrush.

Yield: about 22 cookies

SHINING STAR SHORTBREAD

2 cups butter, softened
1 cup granulated sugar
1/4 teaspoon vanilla extract
4 1/2 cups all-purpose flour
1/4 teaspoon salt
Sparkling sugar crystals

In a mixing bowl, beat butter at medium speed of an electric mixer until creamy; gradually add 1 cup granulated sugar, beating well. Stir in vanilla.

Combine flour and salt; gradually add to butter mixture, beating at low speed after each addition.

Preheat oven to 275 degrees. On a lightly floured surface, use a floured rolling pin to roll out half of dough to 1/2-inch thickness. Cut with a 3-inch star-shaped cookie cutter and place 2 inches apart on ungreased baking sheets. Sprinkle with sugar crystals.

Bake 45 minutes or until edges begin to brown. Transfer cookies to wire racks to cool.

Yield: about 2 1/2 dozen cookies

Gingerbread Snowflake Cookies, Christmas Cookie S'Mores

GINGERBREAD SNOWFLAKE COOKIES

The Royal Icing atop these cookies dries rapidly. Work quickly, keeping extra icing covered tightly at all times.

COOKIES
  1 cup butter or margarine, softened
  1 cup granulated sugar
  ¼ cup water
  1½ teaspoons baking soda
  1 cup molasses
  5 cups all-purpose flour
  ¼ teaspoon salt
  1½ tablespoons ground ginger
  1½ teaspoons ground cinnamon
  ½ teaspoon ground allspice
    Edible white glitter OR granulated sugar (optional)

ROYAL ICING
  1 package (16 ounces) confectioners sugar
  3 tablespoons meringue powder
  6 to 8 tablespoons warm water

For cookies, beat butter and granulated sugar at medium speed of an electric mixer until fluffy (3 to 4 minutes).

Stir together ¼ cup water and baking soda until dissolved; stir in molasses.

Combine flour and next 4 ingredients. Alternately beat dry ingredients and molasses mixture into butter mixture, beginning and ending with flour mixture. Shape mixture into a ball; cover and chill one hour. Divide dough into fourths; work with one piece at a time.

Preheat oven to 350 degrees. On a lightly floured surface, use a floured rolling pin to roll out dough to ¼-inch thickness. Cut with a 3¾-inch snowflake-shaped cookie cutter. Place 2 inches apart on parchment paper-lined baking sheets. Cut out designs in snowflakes using ¼- to ½-inch canapé cutters; transfer cookies to baking sheet. Bake 10 to 12 minutes. Transfer cookies to a wire rack to cool.

For Royal Icing, beat confectioners sugar, meringue powder, and 6 tablespoons warm water at low speed of an electric mixer until blended. Beat at high speed 4 minutes or until stiff peaks form. If needed, add additional water, ¼ teaspoon at a time, to reach desired piping consistency.

Spoon icing into a pastry bag fitted with a small round tip. Pipe icing around edges of cookies. Sprinkle icing with glitter or granulated sugar.
Yield: about 27 cookies
Note: Meringue powder can be found at crafts stores and cake decorating stores.

CHRISTMAS COOKIE S'MORES

Enjoy this holiday cookie version of the favorite campfire treat in the comfort of your own home. Our rendition has a chunky peanut butter crust that's layered with marshmallow creme, chocolate candy, and peanuts.

  ½ cup butter or margarine, softened
  ½ cup granulated sugar
  ½ cup firmly packed brown sugar
  ½ cup crunchy peanut butter
  1 large egg
  ½ teaspoon vanilla extract
  1½ cups all-purpose flour
  2 teaspoons baking powder
  ½ teaspoon salt
  1 jar (7 ounces) marshmallow creme
  1 cup holiday candy-coated chocolate pieces
  ¾ cup salted roasted peanuts

Preheat oven to 375 degrees. In a mixing bowl, beat butter at medium speed of an electric mixer until creamy; add sugars, beating well. Add peanut butter, egg, and vanilla; beat well.

Combine flour, baking powder, and salt; add to butter mixture, beating well.

Press dough into a greased 9 x 13-inch pan. Spread marshmallow creme over dough. Sprinkle chocolate pieces and peanuts over marshmallow creme. Bake 18 to 20 minutes or until marshmallow creme is lightly browned. Cool completely in pan on a wire rack; cut into bars.
Yield: about 2 dozen cookies

WHITE CHOCOLATE-ORANGE DREAM COOKIES

1 cup butter or margarine, softened
⅔ cup firmly packed light brown sugar
½ cup granulated sugar
1 large egg
1 tablespoon grated orange zest
2 teaspoons orange extract
2¼ cups all-purpose flour
¾ teaspoon baking soda
½ teaspoon salt
1 package (12 ounces) white chocolate chips

Preheat oven to 350 degrees. In a mixing bowl, beat first 3 ingredients at medium speed of an electric mixer until creamy. Add egg, orange zest, and orange extract, beating until blended.

Combine flour, baking soda, and salt; gradually add to sugar mixture, beating just until blended after each addition. Stir in chips. Drop dough by rounded tablespoonfuls onto ungreased baking sheets. Bake 10 to 12 minutes or until edges are lightly browned. Cool on baking sheets 2 minutes; transfer to wire racks to cool completely.
Yield: about 3½ dozen cookies

CHOCOLATE-DIPPED PEANUT ROUNDS

½ cup butter or margarine, softened
1 cup firmly packed brown sugar
1 cup smooth peanut butter
1 egg
1 teaspoon vanilla extract
1¼ cups all-purpose flour
¼ teaspoon baking powder
¼ teaspoon baking soda
¼ teaspoon salt
¾ cup coarsely ground peanuts
4 ounces chocolate candy coating, chopped
6 ounces semisweet baking chocolate, chopped

Preheat oven to 350 degrees. In a large mixing bowl, beat butter, brown sugar, and peanut butter at medium

White Chocolate-Orange Dream Cookies, Chocolate-Dipped Peanut Rounds

speed of an electric mixer until fluffy. Add egg and vanilla; beat until smooth.

In a medium bowl, combine flour, baking powder, baking soda, and salt. Add dry ingredients to butter mixture; stir until a soft dough forms. Stir in peanuts. Roll dough into 1-inch balls and place about 2 inches apart on lightly greased baking sheets. Flatten balls into 2-inch-diameter cookies. Bake 11 to 13 minutes or until bottoms are browned. Cool cookies

on baking sheets on wire racks 2 minutes; transfer to a wire rack to cool completely.

In top of a double boiler, melt candy coating and baking chocolate over hot, not simmering, water. Dip half of each cookie into chocolate. Place on waxed paper-lined baking sheets. Chill 15 minutes or until chocolate is firm. Store in a single layer in an airtight container.
Yield: about 5½ dozen cookies

smooth layer, if desired. Cover and chill at least 30 minutes. Cut into 1 x 2-inch bars.
Yield: 32 bars

CHRISTMAS CRINKLES

A drizzle of warm chocolate and a dusting of crushed peppermint candy elevate these white chocolate wafers to Christmas cookie-swap status.

- 4 ounces white baking chocolate, coarsely chopped
- 1/3 cup butter or margarine, softened
- 1 1/2 cups sugar, divided
- 1/4 cup buttermilk
- 1 teaspoon vanilla extract
- 1 large egg
- 2 cups all-purpose flour
- 1/2 teaspoon baking soda
- 1/4 teaspoon salt
- 1/2 cup semisweet chocolate chips
- 1 tablespoon vegetable shortening
  Crushed hard peppermint candy

In a heavy small saucepan, melt white chocolate over low heat, stirring constantly. Remove from heat; set aside.

In a large mixing bowl, beat butter at medium speed of an electric mixer until creamy; gradually add 1 cup sugar, beating well. Add melted white chocolate, buttermilk, vanilla, and egg, beating well.

Combine flour, baking soda, and salt; gradually add to butter mixture, beating well. Cover dough and chill one hour.

Preheat oven to 375 degrees. Shape dough into 1-inch balls; roll balls in remaining 1/2 cup sugar. Place 2 inches apart on ungreased baking sheets. Bake 7 to 8 minutes or until bottoms of cookies are lightly browned. Cool slightly on baking sheets; transfer to wire racks to cool completely.

In a small saucepan, cook chocolate chips and shortening over low heat, stirring constantly, until chocolate and shortening melt. Drizzle mixture evenly over cookies; sprinkle immediately with crushed candy.
Yield: about 6 dozen cookies

Chocolate-Peppermint Bars, Christmas Crinkles

CHOCOLATE-PEPPERMINT BARS

A peppermint filling and chocolate glaze dress up these rich-and-gooey brownies. It's best to chill them before cutting them into bars.

- 1/2 cup plus 3 tablespoons butter or margarine, divided
- 4 1/2 ounces unsweetened baking chocolate, divided
- 1 cup granulated sugar
- 2 large eggs, lightly beaten
- 1/2 cup all-purpose flour
  Dash of salt
- 1 teaspoon peppermint extract, divided
  Few drops red or green liquid food coloring
- 1 1/2 cups confectioners sugar
- 2 to 3 tablespoons whipping cream or half-and-half

Preheat oven to 350 degrees. In a large saucepan, combine 1/2 cup butter and 2 ounces chocolate; cook over low heat until butter and chocolate melt, stirring occasionally. Gradually add granulated sugar and next 3 ingredients, stirring until blended. Stir in 1/4 teaspoon peppermint extract.

Pour batter into a lightly greased 8-inch square pan. Bake 24 minutes. Cool completely in pan on a wire rack.

In a saucepan, melt 2 tablespoons butter over low heat; stir in remaining 3/4 teaspoon peppermint extract, food coloring, confectioners sugar, and whipping cream. Spread over brownies. Chill 15 minutes.

In a small saucepan, combine remaining 1 tablespoon butter and remaining 2 1/2 ounces chocolate; melt over low heat, stirring occasionally. Drizzle chocolate mixture evenly over powdered sugar mixture; spread into a

104

PECAN BISCOTTI

1¾ cups all-purpose flour
1 cup finely chopped pecans
½ cup yellow cornmeal
1¼ teaspoons baking powder
¼ teaspoon salt
¾ cup sugar
½ cup vegetable oil
2 large eggs
⅛ teaspoon almond extract
½ cup semisweet chocolate chips
   (optional)

Preheat oven to 350 degrees. In a large bowl, combine first 5 ingredients. Combine sugar and next 3 ingredients; gradually add to flour mixture, stirring just until dry ingredients are moistened.

Place dough on a lightly floured surface; divide in half. With lightly floured hands, shape each portion of dough into a 2 x 9-inch log. Place logs 3 inches apart on a lightly greased baking sheet. Bake 25 minutes. Cool completely.

Cut each log diagonally into ¾-inch slices, using a serrated knife. Place slices, cut sides down, on ungreased baking sheets. Bake 15 minutes, turning cookies once. Cool cookies slightly on baking sheets; transfer to wire racks to cool completely. If desired, in a small microwave-safe bowl, melt chocolate chips on medium power (50%) 2 minutes and 15 seconds or until chips soften, stirring frequently until smooth. Dip one end of biscotti in chocolate and let cool completely.
Yield: about 21 cookies

Pecan Biscotti

Cranberry Thumbprint Cookies

CRANBERRY THUMBPRINT COOKIES

1 package (6 ounces) sweetened dried cranberries, divided
¾ cup butter or margarine, softened
1 cup sugar
2 eggs
1 teaspoon orange extract
1 teaspoon vanilla extract
2 cups quick-cooking oats
1¾ cups all-purpose flour
1 teaspoon baking powder
¼ teaspoon salt
1 package (12 ounces) white baking chips, divided
1 cup chopped walnuts, toasted

Preheat oven to 350 degrees. Reserve ¼ cup dried cranberries. In a large bowl, beat butter and sugar at medium speed of an electric mixer until fluffy. Add eggs and extracts; beat until smooth. In a medium bowl, combine oats, flour, baking powder, and salt. Add dry ingredients to butter mixture; stir until a soft dough forms. Stir in 1½ cups chips, remaining cranberries, and walnuts.

Shape tablespoonfuls of dough into 1¼-inch balls. Place 2 inches apart on an ungreased baking sheet. Make an indentation in center of each cookie with thumb. Place one reserved cranberry in each indentation. Bake 10 to 12 minutes or until tops are set and bottoms are browned. Transfer cookies to a wire rack with waxed paper underneath to cool.

Place remaining chips in a heavy-duty resealable plastic bag. Microwave on medium power (50%) about 2 minutes or until chips melt. Snip off one corner of bag to create a small opening. Drizzle over cooled cookies. Let drizzle harden. Store in an airtight container.
Yield: about 6 dozen cookies

Strawberry Muffins, Strawberry Butter

GIFTS
FROM HOME

Gifts from your kitchen are gifts from the heart, and they're meant to be shared! Give that special neighbor or teacher a sampling of these goodies all wrapped up especially for them. Strawberry Muffins and their accompanying butter can be enjoyed any time of day, from a quick breakfast to a leisurely bedtime snack. And Cranberry Chutney can double as an appetizer spread over cream cheese or as a condiment for Christmas dinner. There's something for everyone on your list!

STRAWBERRY MUFFINS

1   package (10 ounces) frozen sliced strawberries, thawed and drained
2   cups all-purpose flour
⅔   cup sugar
1   tablespoon baking powder
¾   teaspoon salt
⅔   cup milk
2   large eggs
⅓   cup vegetable oil
    Strawberry Butter to serve

Preheat oven to 375 degrees. Reserve 2 tablespoons sliced strawberries for Strawberry Butter.

In a large bowl, combine flour and next 3 ingredients; make a well in center of mixture. In a medium bowl, combine remaining sliced strawberries, milk, eggs, and oil until blended; add to dry ingredients, stirring just until moistened. Fill lightly greased muffin cups about two-thirds full. Bake 20 minutes. Remove muffins from pans immediately. Serve warm with Strawberry Butter.
Yield: about 16 muffins

STRAWBERRY BUTTER

½   cup butter, softened
2   tablespoons strawberries, reserved from Strawberry Muffins

Combine butter and reserved strawberries until well blended.
Yield: ½ cup strawberry butter

Toy Soldier Surprise
You will need a 5" dia. x 2" tall round papier-mâché box with lid; 4½"w x 14" tall rectangular papier-mâché box with lid; white, flesh tone, pink, red, blue, gold, and black acrylic paint; paintbrushes; iridescent glitter spray; tracing paper; transfer paper; black paint pen; clear acrylic spray sealer; tissue paper; and fabric.

Refer to Painting Techniques, page 156, before beginning project. Allow paint, glitter spray, paint pen, and sealer to dry after each application.

1. Paint round lid black, round box flesh tone, rectangular lid blue, and rectangular box red. Spray round lid with glitter.
2. Trace patterns, pages 122 and 123, onto tracing paper. Use transfer paper to transfer face to round box, arm on each side of rectangular box, and uniform front and shoes on front of rectangular box.
3. Paint face, hands, sleeves, uniform front, and shoes. Add white highlights to eyes and shoes. Use gold paint to add military details (such as fringe and buttons) to uniform. Use paint pen to outline uniform and hands and to add details.
4. Apply two coats of sealer to boxes and lids.
5. Fill rectangular box with tissue paper and Strawberry Muffins. Place Strawberry Butter in a small airtight container; place a piece of fabric and container in round box. Place lids on boxes; stack head on body.

Parmesan Cheese Bites

PARMESAN CHEESE BITES

You can freeze baked cheese bites up to one month.

  1   cup all-purpose flour
  ⅔   cup grated Parmesan cheese
  ¼   teaspoon ground red pepper
  ½   cup butter or margarine,
       cut up
  2   tablespoons milk

In a medium bowl, combine first 3 ingredients. Using a pastry blender or 2 knives, cut butter into dry ingredients until mixture is crumbly. (Mixture will look very dry.) Gently press mixture together with hands, working until blended and smooth (about 2 to 3 minutes). Shape dough into two 4-inch-long logs. Wrap in plastic wrap and place in an airtight container. Chill 8 hours or freeze up to 3 months. (Thaw overnight in refrigerator.)

Preheat oven to 350 degrees. Cut dough into ⅜-inch-thick slices and place on a lightly greased baking sheet. Brush with milk. Bake 12 to 15 minutes or until lightly browned. Remove pan to a wire rack and cool completely. Freeze up to one month, if desired.
Yield: about 32 cheese bites

Fabric-Covered Container
You will need a cardboard chip container with lid, fabric, spray adhesive, 1"w sheer ribbon, sprig of artificial berries with leaves, and a hot glue gun.

1. Measure around container; add ½". Measure height of container between rims. Cut a piece from fabric the determined measurements. Apply spray adhesive to wrong side of fabric. Overlapping edges, smooth fabric around container.
2. Tie two lengths of ribbon into a bow around berry sprig; glue to lid.

A CRANBERRY SENSATION

Cranberry Chutney

CRANBERRY CHUTNEY

½ medium onion, chopped
1 clove garlic, minced
½ jalapeño pepper, seeded
  and chopped
1 slice (½-inch-thick) fresh ginger,
  peeled and chopped
2 tablespoons white wine vinegar
½ teaspoon grated lime zest
1 tablespoon freshly squeezed
  lime juice
2 cans (16 ounces each) whole
  berry cranberry sauce
¼ cup sugar

In a medium saucepan, cook first
7 ingredients over medium-high heat,
stirring constantly, 10 to 15 minutes or
until mixture is tender. Stir in cranberry
sauce and sugar; bring to a boil.
Remove from heat. Cover and chill
2 hours. Store in refrigerator up to
2 weeks. Serve with gingersnaps or as
a condiment for pork or poultry.
Yield: about 3½ cups chutney

Frosted Snowflake Jar
You will need snowflake stickers,
clear glass jar with lid, aluminum foil,
frosted glass spray finish, iridescent
glitter paint, small paintbrush, and
1 yd. of white sheer ribbon.

1. Adhere snowflakes to jar as desired.
2. Cover jar opening with foil. Follow
manufacturer's instructions to paint jar
with frosted finish; allow to dry.
Remove snowflakes and foil.
3. Paint top and sides of lid with glitter
paint; allow to dry.
4. Tie ribbon into a bow around neck
of jar; trim ends.

JALAPEÑO PIMIENTO CHEESE

Pimiento cheese is anything but ordinary when you stir in flecks of jalapeño pepper.

- 1 container (8 ounces) pasteurized process cheese spread, cubed
- 1 package (8 ounces) shredded three-cheese gourmet Cheddar cheese blend
- 1 package (8 ounces) shredded sharp Cheddar cheese
- 1½ tablespoons sugar
- ¼ teaspoon salt
- ¼ teaspoon ground black pepper
- 1 jar (4 ounces) diced pimientos, drained
- 2 jalapeño peppers, seeded and minced
- 1 cup mayonnaise
  Crackers or pear wedges to serve

Process half of cheeses in a food processor until smooth, stopping to scrape down sides. Transfer to a bowl.

Process remaining cheeses, sugar, salt, and black pepper in food processor until smooth, stopping to scrape down sides. Stir into cheese mixture in bowl; stir in pimientos, jalapeño peppers, and mayonnaise. Spoon into half-pint jars and store in refrigerator. Serve with crackers or pear wedges.

Yield: about 1 quart pimiento cheese

Cheese Pizzazz

You will need corn husks, rubber bands, red ribbon, red and green cloth napkins, 12" dia. terra-cotta saucer, pears, and crackers.

1. For each jar, soak several husks in water until pliable. Cover lid with husks; secure with a rubber band. Knot a length of ribbon over rubber band.
2. Line saucer with red and green napkins, then fill with pears, crackers, and covered jars.

Jalapeño Pimiento Cheese

Brazil Nut Coins

BRAZIL NUT COINS

1 cup butter or margarine, softened
½ cup firmly packed brown sugar
½ cup granulated sugar
2 eggs
1 teaspoon vanilla extract
2 cups all-purpose flour
½ teaspoon ground cinnamon
¼ teaspoon ground nutmeg
⅛ teaspoon ground cloves
1½ cups coarsely ground Brazil nuts

In a large bowl, beat butter and sugars until fluffy. Add eggs and vanilla; beat until smooth. In a small bowl, combine flour, cinnamon, nutmeg, and cloves. Add dry ingredients to butter mixture; stir until a soft dough forms. Stir in Brazil nuts. Shape dough into three 8-inch-long rolls. Wrap rolls in plastic wrap and chill 2 hours or until firm.

Preheat oven to 350 degrees. Cut dough into ¼-inch-thick slices. Place one inch apart on ungreased baking sheets. Bake 9 to 11 minutes or until edges are lightly browned. Transfer cookies to wire racks to cool. Store in an airtight container.
Yield: about 6 dozen cookies

Christmas Poppers
You will need white card stock, plastic food wrap, transparent tape, decorative-edge craft scissors, tissue paper, curling ribbon, corrugated craft cardboard, and wrapping paper.

1. For each popper, wrap a piece of card stock around a 6" long stack of plastic-wrapped cookies; secure with tape.
2. Use craft scissors to cut a 14" x 20" piece from tissue paper. Center tube along one short end of tissue. Roll tissue around tube and secure with tape. Tie each end with ribbon.
3. Measure around tube; add ½". Use craft scissors to cut a 3½"w piece from cardboard, and a 3"w piece from wrapping paper the determined measurement. Overlapping ends at back and securing with tape, wrap cardboard, then wrapping paper around popper.

Dream Creams

Chocolate-Lemon Creams

CHOCOLATE-LEMON CREAMS

2 packages (8 ounces each) cream cheese, softened
1 cup confectioners sugar
2 tablespoons grated lemon zest
3 tablespoons freshly squeezed lemon juice
1 teaspoon lemon extract
24 ounces chocolate candy coating, chopped
4 ounces white candy coating (optional), chopped

In a medium bowl, beat first 5 ingredients until smooth; cover. Freeze 2 hours.

Shape cream cheese mixture into 1-inch balls and place on a waxed paper-lined baking sheet; cover and freeze one hour. Let stand at room temperature 10 minutes.

In a 1-quart microwave-safe bowl, microwave chocolate candy coating on high power (100%) 1½ minutes or until coating melts, stirring twice.

Dip balls into chocolate coating; place on waxed paper. Let stand until coating is firm.

Place white coating in a resealable plastic bag. Seal and submerge coating in warm water until melted. Snip a tiny hole in one corner of bag and drizzle coating over chocolates, if desired.
Yield: about 6 dozen candies

Beaded Box

You will need foam brushes, dark red acrylic paint, 5" dia. papier-mâché box with lid, green bugle beads, thin jewelry wire, wire cutters, thick tacky glue, red and green seed beads, a mixture of light green seed beads and iridescent seed and bugle beads, and eighteen red beads for berries.

Allow paint and glue to dry after each application.

1. Paint box and lid red.
2. Thread approximately twenty green bugle beads onto an 8" length of wire. Twist ends together to form a tight circle of beads; do not trim wire ends. Using pattern, page 122, form circle into leaf shape. Thread eight bugle beads onto one end of wire; bend end up to form vein at center of leaf. Twist end of wire around top of leaf to secure; trim ends of wire. Repeat to make five more leaves.
3. Apply glue along rim of lid. While glue is still wet, roll rim of lid through red seed beads until lid is covered completely.
4. Apply glue to top of lid. While glue is still wet, arrange leaves on lid; fill in each leaf with green seed beads. Glue three berry beads between each leaf. Cover remainder of lid with bead mixture.

SWEET AND SPICY

LITTLE CINNAMON SWIRL LOAVES

1 package (18¼ ounces) yellow cake mix with pudding in the mix
4 large eggs
¾ cup vegetable oil
¾ cup water
1 teaspoon vanilla extract
½ cup sugar
3 tablespoons ground cinnamon

Preheat oven to 350 degrees. In a large bowl, beat first 5 ingredients at high speed of an electric mixer 3 minutes. Pour half of batter evenly into 5 greased and floured 3¼ x 6-inch aluminum foil loaf pans. Combine sugar and cinnamon; sprinkle half of sugar mixture evenly over batter in pans. Pour remaining batter evenly into pans and sprinkle evenly with remaining sugar mixture. Gently swirl with a knife. Bake 35 minutes or until a toothpick inserted in center loaf comes out clean. Cool in pans on wire racks. Store in freezer, if desired.
Yield: 5 loaves

Festive Wrapping

For each loaf, you will need a 1-gallon plastic bag, wire-edged ribbon, large cinnamon stick, and a sprig of artificial holly with berries.

1. Place loaf in plastic bag.
2. Tie ribbon into a bow around top of bag. Tuck cinnamon stick and holly sprig behind bow.

Little Cinnamon Swirl Loaves

EARTHLY GRANDEUR

TRIO OF TREES
(Shown on pages 8 and 9)

For each tree, you will need sand; 48"h, 60"h, or 72"h artificial evergreen tree with removable stand; 17½"h x 19" dia. or 20"h x 25" dia. rusted cast-iron urn; Spanish moss; grapevine garland; floral wire; wire cutters; silk amaryllis stalks; juniper sprigs; assorted artificial leaves; assorted red berry sprigs; and a hot glue gun.

1. Using sand, "plant" tree in urn; cover sand with moss.
2. Unwind grapevine and wrap around tree; wire in place. Cut stalk to 4" on each amaryllis. Inserting stems into grapevine, arrange juniper sprigs, leaves, berry sprigs, and amaryllis along grapevine; glue or wire items in place.

BANISTER ROPING
(Shown on page 12)

You will need a grapevine garland, artificial Canadian pine garland, floral wire, wire cutters, juniper sprigs, assorted artificial leaves and red berry sprigs, hot glue gun, and Seeded Star Ornaments (this page).

1. Unwind grapevine and wrap around pine garland; wire in place. Inserting stems into grapevine, arrange juniper sprigs, leaves, and berry sprigs along grapevine; glue or wire items in place.
2. Glue Seeded Star Ornaments to garland as desired.

NATURAL CANDLE ARRANGEMENT
(Shown on page 13)

You will need a hot glue gun, 12" dia. foam disk, 15" dia. galvanized charger, sheet moss, three pillar candles in assorted heights, clump moss, juniper sprigs, pinecones, reindeer moss, red berry sprigs, Seeded Star Ornament (this page), and star anise.

1. For base, center and glue foam disk on charger. Glue sheet moss over base, covering top and sides of disk and top of charger completely.
2. Center and glue candles on base.
3. Arrange and glue clump moss, juniper sprigs, pinecones, reindeer moss, and berry sprigs on base around candles.
4. Glue Seeded Star Ornament, then star anise to base.

SEEDED STAR ORNAMENTS
(Shown on page 12)

For each ornament, you will need craft glue, 4" dia. papier-mâché star ornament, rye grass seed, star anise (optional), and a hot glue gun (optional).

1. Apply craft glue to one side of papier-mâché star, dip into rye grass seed until completely covered, and allow to dry. Repeat to cover other side of star.
2. If desired, hot glue a star anise to one point of star.

TABLETOP TOPIARIES
(Shown on page 10)

For each topiary, you will need floral foam, utility knife, craft stick, craft glue, foam brush, sheet moss, hot glue gun, reindeer moss, star anise, and artificial red berry sprigs.

For small topiary, you will need a 5"h x 4" dia. cast-iron urn and a 6"h foam cone.

For medium topiary, you will need a 5"h x 4" dia. cast-iron urn, 9"h foam cone, and preserved cedar sprigs.

For large topiary, you will need a 6"h x 5½" dia. cast-iron urn, 12"h foam cone, grapevine garland, and preserved cedar sprigs.

Use hot glue for all gluing unless otherwise indicated. Allow craft glue to dry after each application.

1. For each topiary, fill urn with foam to 1" from top. Insert craft stick into bottom of foam cone, then into foam in urn. Use craft glue to glue sheet moss over cone, covering cone completely.
2. For small topiary, glue small pieces of reindeer moss to topiary as desired. Glue one star anise and one berry to each moss piece.
3. For medium topiary, glue a garland of reindeer moss around topiary. Glue cedar sprigs, berries, and star anise along garland.
4. For large topiary, wrap several lengths of garland around topiary; glue in place. Glue reindeer moss, cedar sprigs, and berries to top and front of topiary. Glue star anise to topiary as desired.

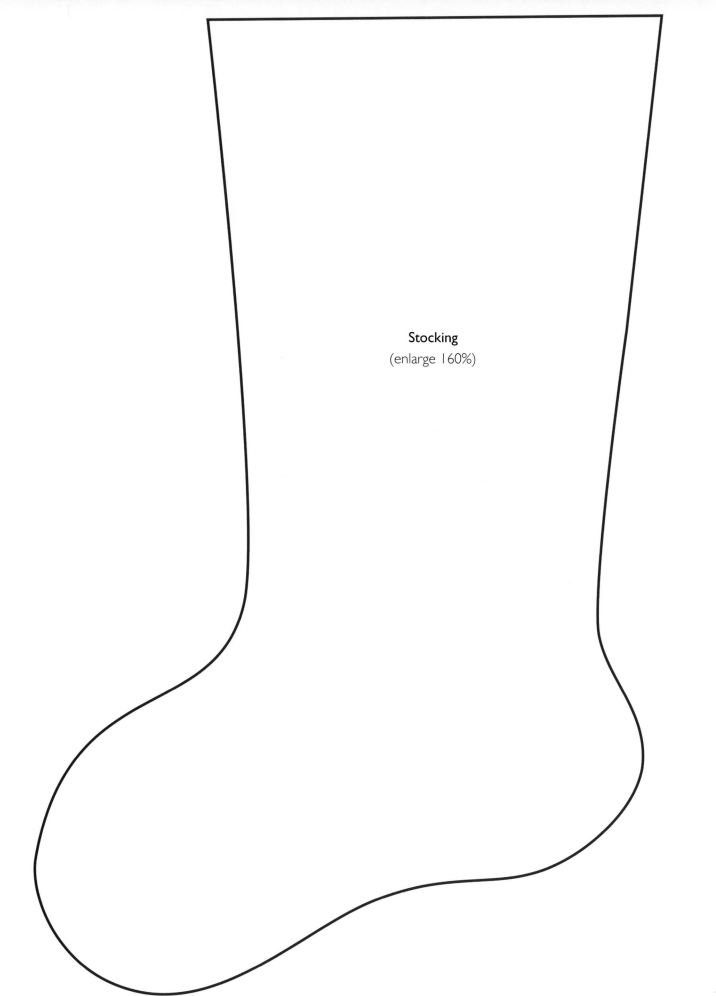

Stocking
(enlarge 160%)

FRUITFUL OPULENCE

BOUNTIFUL TOPIARIES
(Shown on page 14)

For each topiary, you will need a 6" dia. x 12"h foam cone topiary, 8"h ceramic urn (ours came painted with a bronze-patina finish), floral picks, floral foam, craft glue, sheet moss, greenery pins, artificial evergreen sprigs and leaves (we used flocked juniper, Reno pine, and Sisal leaves), gold and copper berry sprigs, beaded fruit (we used an apple, a fig, a pomegranate, two plums, three pears, and grape clusters), and a hot glue gun.

Allow craft glue to dry after each application.

1. Trim base of topiary to fit in urn; remove from urn and insert two floral picks in bottom of base. Fill urn with enough floral foam so top of topiary base is even with rim of urn; place topiary in urn.
2. Use craft glue to attach sheet moss over cone and base, covering completely.
3. Use greenery pins to attach evergreen and leaves to base and cone; add berry sprigs to cone. Glue beaded fruit to topiary as desired.

FRUIT TOPIARIES
(Shown on page 16)

For each topiary, you will need a 2"h or 4"h clay pot, gold spray paint, gold acrylic paint, natural sponge piece, floral foam, utility knife, 5" to 6" long straight twig, craft glue, foam brush, sheet moss, 14" length of ³/₄"w wire-edged ribbon, piece of beaded fruit (for our topiaries, we used pears, apples, pomegranates, and plums), and a hot glue gun.

Allow paint and craft glue to dry after each application.

1. For each topiary, spray pot gold. *Sponge Paint*, page 156, pot with gold acrylic paint.
2. Fill pot with foam to ¹/₂" from top. Insert twig into bottom of fruit, then into foam in pot. Use craft glue to attach sheet moss over foam in pot, covering completely.
3. Tie ribbon into a bow around twig; notch ends.

FRAMED PRINTS
(Shown on page 14)

For each print, you will need a color photocopy of desired print (page 117) on white card stock and a gold frame to fit 3" x 5" print.

1. Cut out photocopy along grey lines.
2. If desired, remove stand from back of frame. Mount print in frame.

Leisure Arts, Inc., grants permission to the owner of this book to photocopy the print designs on page 117 for personal use only.

117

NOBLE ESTATE

SHIELD ORNAMENTS
(Shown on page 20)

For each ornament, you will need tracing paper, cardboard, black velveteen, plaid and solid red wool fabrics, spray adhesive, hot glue gun, $1/8$" and $1/4$" dia. gold cord, 3" long gold tassel, and a $7/8$" dia. gold crest-embossed button.

Use hot glue for all gluing unless otherwise indicated.

1. Trace patterns A, B, and C, page 120, onto tracing paper; cut out. Draw around Pattern A once on cardboard and twice on wrong side of velveteen. Draw around Pattern B once on wrong side of red fabric and Pattern C once on wrong side of plaid fabric. Cut out cardboard, red fabric, and plaid fabric pieces along drawn lines. Cut out one velveteen piece $1/4$" inside drawn line and remaining velveteen piece $1/2$" outside drawn line.
2. Apply spray adhesive to wrong side of larger velveteen piece; center and smooth onto cardboard. Clipping corners as needed, wrap edges to back.
3. Apply spray adhesive to wrong sides of B and C pieces; arrange and smooth on front of ornament. Beginning and ending at bottom and gluing ends to back, glue $1/8$" dia. cord along edges of ornament.
4. For hanger, cut an 8" length of $1/4$" dia. cord; glue ends of cord at top corners on back of ornament. Center and glue hanger of tassel on back of ornament with tassel close to point.
5. Glue remaining velveteen piece over back of ornament. Glue button at center on front of ornament.

ARISTOCRATIC PILLOWS
(Shown on page 20)

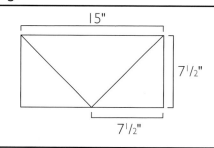

ENVELOPE PILLOW

You will need two $7^1/2$" x 15" pieces of black velveteen for flap, gold thread, $2/3$ yd. of $1/4$" dia. gold cord, two 15" squares of plaid wool fabric for pillow front and back, 14" square pillow form, 2" long gold tassel with hanger, and a $7/8$" dia. gold crest-embossed shank button.

Use a $1/2$" seam allowance for all sewing.

1. For flap, refer to Fig. 1 to cut one triangle from each velveteen fabric piece.

Fig. 1

15"

$7^1/2$"

$7^1/2$"

2. Use gold thread to stitch a length of cord 1" from edges of point on one flap piece. Matching right sides and leaving long edges open for turning, sew edges of point together to form flap; clip point and turn flap right side out.
3. Matching raw edges, baste flap to one edge (top) of one pillow square. Matching right sides and leaving bottom edge open for turning, sew

pillow squares together. Clip corners, turn right side out, and press. Insert pillow form and sew opening closed.
4. Sew tassel and button to point of flap.

THROW PILLOW

You will need paper-backed fusible web, black felt, black velveteen, plaid and solid red wool fabrics, two 11" squares of red wool fabric for pillow front and back, clear nylon thread, gold thread, $1^1/2$ yds. of $1/4$" dia. gold cord, $7/8$" dia. crest-embossed gold button, and a 10" square pillow form.

Use a $1/2$" seam allowance for all sewing.

1. Using patterns, page 120, follow *Fusible Appliques*, page 154, to make one A appliqué each from felt and velveteen, one B appliqué from red fabric, and one C appliqué from plaid fabric for shield.
2. Center and fuse felt, then velveteen appliqués on one pillow fabric square. Arrange and fuse remaining appliqués on shield. Using clear thread, follow *Machine Appliqué*, page 154, to sew along outer edge of shield.
3. Beginning and ending at bottom, use gold thread to stitch cord along outer edge of shield. Sew button at center of shield.
4. Matching rights sides and leaving bottom edge open for turning, sew pillow squares together. Clip corners, turn right side out, and press. Insert pillow form and sew opening closed.
5. Forming a small loop in cord at each corner of pillow, use gold thread to stitch cord along edges of pillow.

FLEECE THROW WITH GILDED SHIELD

(Shown on page 20)

You will need plaid wool fabric for facing, 1²/₃ yd. piece of fleece, paper-backed fusible web, black felt, black velveteen, plaid and solid red wool fabrics, assorted coordinating trims, clear nylon thread, gold thread, 1¹/₂ yds. of ¹/₄" dia. gold cord, 2" long gold tassel, and a ⁷/₈" dia. gold crest-embossed shank button for shield.

Use a ¹/₂" seam allowance for all sewing.

1. Cut a 28" square from fabric. Follow *Making a Continuous Bias Strip*, page 154, to make a 3"w strip from square. For facings, cut two 62" and two 65" lengths from strip; press one long edge of each length ¹/₂" to wrong side.

2. Matching raw edges and back of fleece to right side of facing, pin 62" facings to side edges of fleece; sew in place. Trim ends even with fleece. Press facings out, then press seam toward facing.

3. Repeat Step 2 to sew 65" facings to top and bottom edges of throw.

4. Press corners of facings diagonally, matching corners of facing to corners of fleece (Fig. 1).

Fig. 1

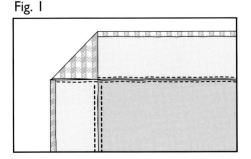

5. Pin facings to front, mitering corners; topstitch edges and corners to secure.

Fig. 2

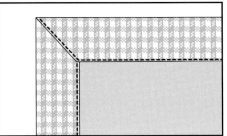

6. Using patterns, page 121, follow *Fusible Appliqués*, page 154, to make one X appliqué each from felt and velveteen, one Y appliqué from red fabric, and one Z appliqué from plaid fabric.

7. Center and fuse felt, then velveteen appliqués on one corner of throw. Arrange and fuse remaining appliqués on shield. Using clear thread, follow *Machine Appliqué*, page 154, to sew along outer edge of shield.

8. Trimming ends to fit, use gold thread to stitch lengths of trim over inner edges of shield.

9. Beginning and ending at bottom, use gold thread to stitch cord along outer edge of shield. Sew tassel, then button to point of shield.

PLAID STOCKINGS

(Shown on page 21)

For each stocking, you will need two 12" x 20" pieces of wool fabric for stocking front and back (we used plaid for stocking front and solid red for stocking back), 20" x 24" piece of fabric for lining, tracing paper, 15" x 20" piece of black velveteen for cuff, gold thread, ¹/₄" dia. gold cord, 3" long gold tassel, and a ⁷/₈" dia. gold crest-embossed shank button.

Use a ¹/₄" seam allowance for all sewing.

1. For pattern, enlarge stocking pattern, page 115, 160% on copier; cut out pattern.

2. For stocking, place stocking front and stocking back fabrics right sides together. Using pattern, cut out stocking. Leaving top edge open, sew stocking pieces together. Clip curves; turn stocking right side out.

3. Matching right sides and short edges, fold lining fabric in half; use pattern to cut out lining. Leaving top edge open and a 5" opening in center back seamline for turning, sew lining pieces together. Clip curves; do not turn lining right side out.

4. Trace cuff pattern, page 120, onto tracing paper. Matching right sides and short edges, fold cuff fabric piece in half. Use pattern to cut two sets of cuff pieces from fabric.

5. For cuff front, use gold thread to stitch a length of cord ³/₄" from edges of point on right side of one cuff piece.

6. Matching right sides, place two cuff pieces together; sew side edges together. Repeat with remaining cuff pieces.

7. Matching right sides, place cuff pieces together. Leaving top edge open, sew pieces together along points. Clip corners and turn right side out. Matching raw edges, pin cuff to stocking; baste in place.

8. Matching right sides, place stocking into lining (cuff should be between stocking and lining).

9. For hanger, fold a 10" length of cord in half; knot hanger 3" from fold. Matching ends of hanger to top of stocking at heelside seamline, tack hanger in place between stocking and lining.

10. Sew top edges of stocking and lining together, catching ends of hanger in stitching. Turn stocking right side out through opening in lining. Sew opening in lining closed; insert lining into stocking.

11. Sew tassel, then button to point of cuff.

FAUX-LEATHER ORNAMENTS

(Shown on page 20)

For each ornament, you will need a hot glue gun, unfinished wooden cutout to fit on front of ornament, ¹/₄" thick papier-mâché ornament with hanger, light brown and dark brown acrylic paint, paintbrushes, clear satin acrylic spray sealer, and a ⁷/₈" dia. gold crest-embossed button.

Allow paint and sealer to dry after each application.

1. For ornament, center and glue cutout on ornament.

2. Paint ornament light brown. Spray ornament with sealer. Mix one part dark brown paint with two parts water. Brush paint mixture on ornament; use a paper towel to dab surface until desired effect is achieved. Spray ornament with sealer.

3. Glue button to center of ornament.

FAUX-LEATHER CANDLESTICKS

(Shown on page 21)

For each candlestick, you will need a drill and $3/4$" dia. countersink bit, $5^3/4$" to $6^7/8$" tall wooden fence finial, sandpaper, tack cloth, spray primer, light brown and dark brown acrylic paint, paintbrushes, soft cloth, paste floor wax, black craft foam, and craft glue.

Allow primer, paint, and glue to dry after each application.

1. Drill a 1" deep hole in center top of finial. Sand finial and wipe with tack cloth. Spray finial with primer.

2. Paint finial with two coats light brown paint. Mix one part dark brown paint with two parts water. Brush paint mixture on finial; use a paper towel to dab surface until desired effect is achieved.

3. Use soft cloth to apply a thin, even coat of wax to finial, then buff.

4. Draw around bottom of candlestick on craft foam; cut out shape just inside drawn line. Glue shape to bottom of candlestick.

Stocking Cuff

A

C

B

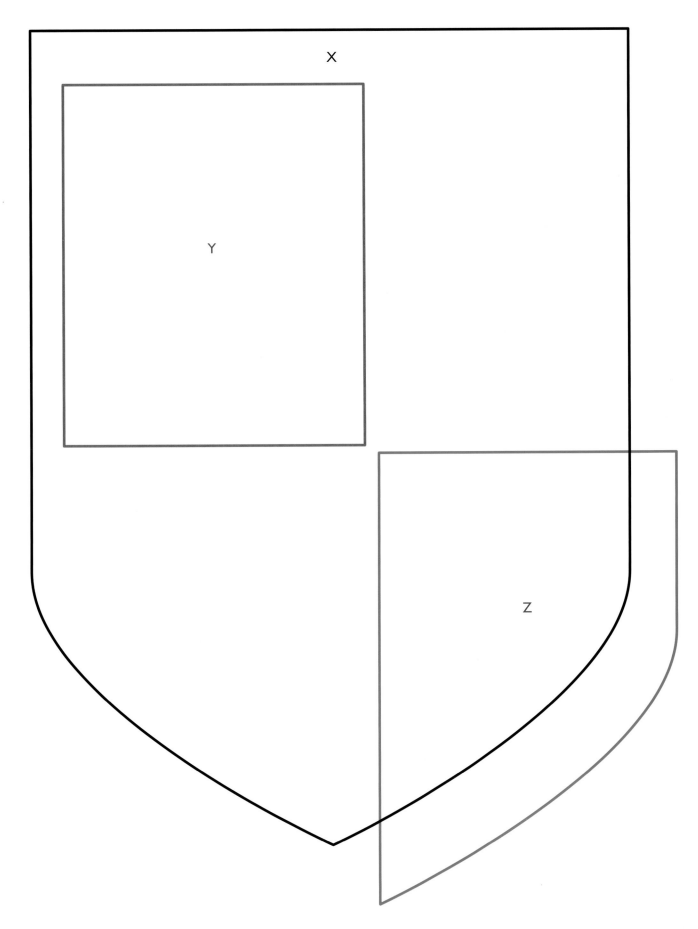

X

Y

Z

Face

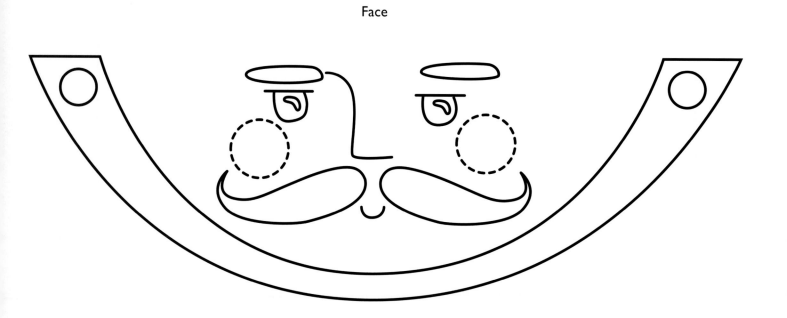

Shoes

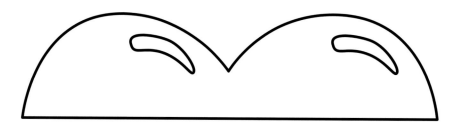

Holly Leaf

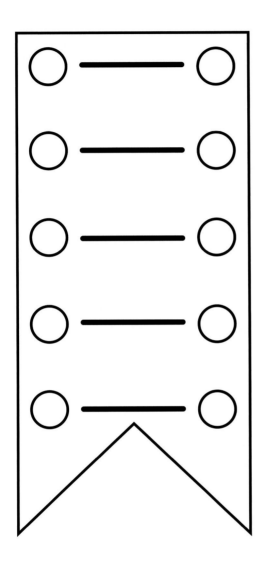

Front

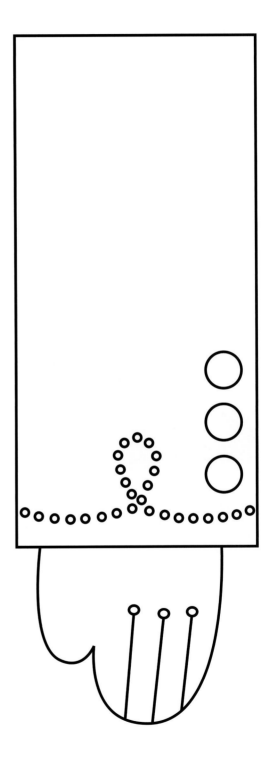

DREAMY WHITE CHRISTMAS

WINTER BERRY WREATH

(Shown on page 24)

You will need cardboard, tacky glue, foam brush, 18" dia. plastic-foam wreath, artificial white berries removed from stems (we used tallow berries), 3"w white wire-edged fabric ribbon, and a picture hanger.

1. For backing, draw around edges of wreath on cardboard; cut out 1/2" inside drawn lines. Glue backing to wreath; allow to dry.
2. Applying glue to wreath, one small area at a time, press berries into glue until wreath is completely covered; allow to dry.
3. Tie ribbon into a bow around top of wreath. Attach hanger to back of wreath.

STUNNING STOCKINGS

(Shown on page 24)

CHENILLE STOCKING

You will need one each 20" x 24" piece of white chenille fabric for stocking and fabric for lining (we used lightweight cotton broadcloth), 1/4" dia. cord for hanger, 7" dia. ecru crocheted doily, and 3/8"w ecru satin ribbon.

Use a 1/4" seam allowance for all sewing.

1. For pattern, enlarge stocking pattern, page 115, 160% on copier; cut out pattern.

2. Matching right sides and short edges, fold stocking and lining fabrics in half; use pattern to cut out stocking and lining from fabrics.
3. Leaving top edge open, sew stocking pieces together; clip curves. Turn stocking right side out. Leaving top edge open and a 5" opening in center back seamline for turning, sew lining pieces together. Clip curves; do not turn lining right side out.
4. Matching right sides, place stocking into lining.
5. For hanger, fold a 7" length of cord in half to form a loop. Matching ends of loop to top of stocking at heelside seamline, tack hanger in place between stocking and lining.
6. Sew top edges of stocking and lining together, catching ends of hanger in stitching. Turn stocking and lining right side out through opening in lining. Sew opening in lining closed. Insert lining into stocking.
7. For decoration, gather doily across center. Wrap thread around gathers several times to secure; knot and trim ends. Tie ribbon into a bow around gathers, leaving long streamers. Arrange doily on front of stocking; tack in place.

VELVET STOCKING

You will need one each 20" x 24" piece of white velvet for stocking and fabric for lining (we used satin), 8 1/2" of 1 1/8"w white cord trim, 1/4" dia. cord for hanger, 1 3/4" dia. covered button kit, fabric to cover button (we used white velvet), and a 7" long white tassel.

Use a 1/4" seam allowance for all sewing.

1. Follow Steps 1 – 3 of Chenille Stocking to cut out and sew stocking and lining pieces together.

2. For cuff flap, cut two 3 3/4" x 8" pieces from velvet. Matching right sides and leaving one long edge unsewn, sew pieces together. Clip corners and turn right side out. Center and tack trim to flap 1 1/2" from raw edges; tack ends to wrong side of flap. Matching raw edges, center and pin flap to stocking front; baste in place.
3. Matching right sides, place stocking into lining (flap should be between stocking and lining).
4. Follow Steps 5 and 6 of Chenille Stocking to attach hanger and complete top of stocking.
5. Follow manufacturer's instructions to cover button with fabric. Sew tassel and button to flap.

SATEEN STOCKING

You will need 20" x 24" piece of sateen fabric for stocking, 20" x 24" piece of fabric for lining (we used satin), 12" square ecru linen napkin with crocheted edging, 1/4" dia. cord for hanger, and assorted off-white buttons.

Use a 1/4" seam allowance for all sewing.

1. Follow Steps 1 – 3 of Chenille Stocking to cut out and sew stocking and lining pieces together.
2. For cuff, fold napkin in half diagonally; cut along fold (you will use only one half of napkin). Matching raw edges, center and pin cuff on stocking; baste in place.
3. Matching right sides, place stocking into lining (cuff should be between stocking and lining).
4. Follow Steps 5 and 6 of Chenille Stocking to attach hanger and complete top of stocking.
5. Sew buttons along top of cuff.

A STERLING YULETIDE TEA

LAYERED TREE SKIRT
(Shown on page 33)

You will need 1¹/₃ yds. of 60"w fabric for top layer of skirt, string, fabric marking pencil, thumbtack, and 1¹/₂ yds. of 60"w fabric for bottom layer of skirt.

1. Fold fabric for top layer of skirt in half from top to bottom and again from left to right.
2. Tie one end of string to pencil. Insert thumbtack through string 23¹/₂" from pencil for outer cutting line. Insert thumbtack through fabric as shown in Fig. 1; mark outer cutting line.

Fig. 1

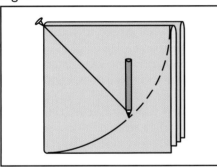

3. Repeat Step 2, inserting thumbtack 2" from pencil for inner cutting line; mark inner cutting line. Cut along drawn lines through all fabric layers.
4. For opening in back of skirt, cut through one layer of fabric along one fold line from outer to inner edge. Press edges of skirt ¹/₄" to wrong side; press ¹/₄" to wrong side again and topstitch in place.
5. For bottom layer of skirt, repeat Steps 1 – 4, using 27¹/₂" for outer cutting line.
6. Arrange bottom skirt, then top skirt around tree.

TASSELED "FROG" ORNAMENTS
(Shown on page 32)

For each tassel ornament, you will need a 27" chair tie with 3" tassels, hot glue gun, 1¹/₈" dia. button cover kit, fabric to cover button, and clear nylon thread.

1. Referring to Fig. 1, form chair tie into three equal loops to make "frog"; glue to secure.

Fig. 1

2. Follow manufacturer's instructions to cover button with fabric. Glue button to center of frog.
3. For hanger, thread 10" of clear thread through back of ornament; knot thread ends together.

FABRIC ROSE ORNAMENTS
(Shown on page 32)

For each rose ornament, you will need fabric, matching heavy-duty thread, 6" of floral wire, green floral tape, hot glue gun, and artificial rose leaves.

1. For each rose, cut a 4¹/₂" x 27" strip from fabric. Work *Running Stitches*, page 157, along one long edge of strip (bottom). Pull threads to gather bottom edge of strip. Matching right sides, fold top of strip diagonally to bottom edge (Fig. 1); wrap fabric tightly for several turns to form rose center; tack in place. Tacking bottom of strip in place as you go, continue wrapping strip around rose center; knot and trim thread at end of strip.

Fig. 1

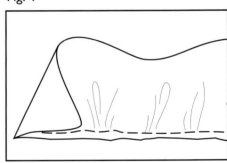

2. Turn top edges of strip to outside to form petals.
3. For stem, wrap wire with tape. Glue one end of stem and leaves to bottom of rose.

CHARMING ANGELS

(Shown on page 32)

For each angel, you will need a 4" x 11" piece of muslin, polyester fiberfill, white chenille stem, hot glue gun, 3" x 10" piece of batting, 2³/₄" vinyl doll arms, 4" vinyl doll head with chest, tracing paper, fabrics for dress, ³/₈"w scallop-edged lace, 27" long chair tie with 3" tassels, craft glue, 4¹/₂"h x 6"w quilted muslin wings, and tissue paper.

Use a ¹/₄" seam allowance for all sewing unless otherwise indicated. Use hot glue for all gluing unless otherwise indicated.

1. For body, match short edges to fold muslin piece in half. Leaving one end open for stuffing, sew edges together; turn right side out and lightly stuff with fiberfill. Work *Running Stitches*, page 157, around open end (top of body). Pull thread ends to gather; knot ends together to secure.

2. For arms, center chenille stem lengthwise on batting piece and glue in place. Roll batting piece tightly around chenille stem; glue to secure. Glue one arm on each end of stem. Center and glue arms to head under shoulders; glue head to body.

3. For bodice, cut a 10" x 16" piece from fabric. Matching short edges, fold fabric in half; fold again from left to right. Referring to Bodice Diagram, draw bodice pattern onto tracing paper; mark edges to place on folds of fabric. Use pattern to cut bodice from fabric. Cut bodice down center back for back opening.

4. Press sleeve edges ¹/₄" to wrong side; stitch in place. Press edges of center back opening ¹/₈" to wrong side; stitch in place. For collar, cut a piece of lace to fit along edge of neck opening. Matching right sides and straight edge of lace to raw edge of neck opening, sew lace in place; press seam to wrong side. Matching right sides and raw edges, sew underarms and side seams of bodice. Turn right side out and press.

5. For waistband, cut a 1¹/₄" x 10¹/₂" strip from fabric. Matching wrong sides, press strip in half.

6. For skirt, cut a 16" x 21" piece from fabric. Fold one long edge ¹/₂" to wrong side; fold ¹/₂" to wrong side again and stitch in place. Work *Running Stitches* ¹/₄" from remaining long edge. Pull thread to gather edge to fit waistband. Matching raw edges, baste skirt to waistband. Matching right sides and raw edges, center and pin bodice to skirt. Sew bodice to skirt; press waistband toward bodice. Matching right sides and raw edges, sew back of skirt closed. Turn dress right side out and place on angel; sew bodice closed.

7. Cut 1" from ends of tassels on chair tie. Center and knot chair tie over waistband.

8. To gather sleeves, use craft glue to attach a piece of lace around each wrist; allow to dry.

9. Glue wings to back of angel. If desired, fill skirt with crumpled tissue paper for fullness.

BODICE DIAGRAM

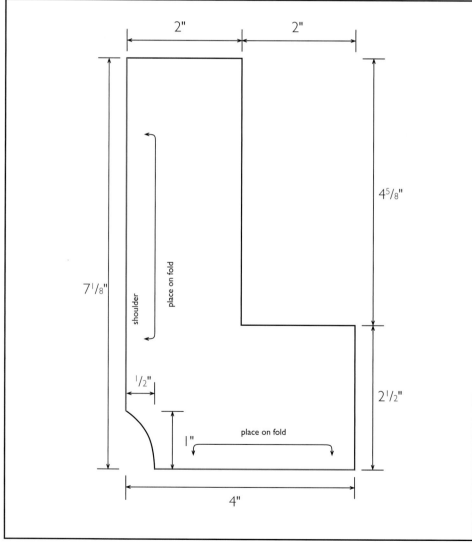

MANTEL SCARF
(Shown on page 34)

You will need fabric, 1"w wired fabric ribbon, 3/16" dia. cord, 1 1/8" dia. button cover kit, fabric to cover buttons, and a hot glue gun.

1. Measure length and width of mantel; add 1" to each measurement. Cut a piece of fabric the determined measurements. Cut a second piece of fabric 7"w by the determined length. Press one long and both short edges of each piece 1/4" to wrong side; press 1/4" to wrong side again and stitch in place.
2. To determine number of tabs needed, divide length of mantel by 14; round down to the nearest whole number. Cut determined number of 4 1/2" lengths of ribbon.
3. Beginning 7" from each end and spacing tabs evenly, pin one end of tabs along raw edge on right side of 7"w fabric piece. Matching edges, wrap free ends of tabs around fabric to form gathers; baste tabs in place.
4. Matching right sides and raw edges, use a 1/2" seam allowance to sew fabric pieces together press seam open.
5. For each "frog," refer to Fig. 1 to form a 12" piece of cord into three equal loops; glue to secure. Follow manufacturer's instructions to cover one button with fabric. Glue covered button to center of frog. Glue frogs to tabs.

Fig. 1

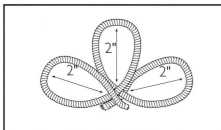

CHRISTMAS MEMORIES JOURNAL
(Shown on page 35)

You will need a hardbound journal, fabrics to cover outside and inside covers of journal, craft glue, 1/2 yd. of 1 1/2"w wired fabric ribbon, 1 yd. of 5/8"w satin ribbon, 12" of 3/16" dia. cord, hot glue gun, 1 1/8" dia. button cover kit, and fabric to cover button.

Use craft glue for all gluing unless otherwise indicated; allow to dry after each application.

1. Draw around open journal on wrong side of fabric; cut out 1 1/2" outside drawn lines. Center open journal on wrong side of fabric piece. Fold corners of fabric diagonally over corners of journal; glue to secure. Trim fabric even with top and bottom of spine. Fold edges of fabric over edges of journal; glue to secure.
2. Gluing ends to inside, glue a length of 1 1/2"w ribbon along opening edge of front cover.
3. For closure, cut two 7" lengths of 5/8"w ribbon. Center and glue one end of one ribbon on opening edge on inside front cover; trim ribbon end. Repeat on back cover.
4. To cover inside of journal, draw around closed journal two times on fabric. Cut out 1/2" inside drawn lines. Center and glue fabric pieces over inside covers. Cut pieces of 5/8"w ribbon to fit along top, bottom, and sides of fabric pieces inside journal. Glue ribbons over fabric pieces, covering raw edges.
5. Gluing ends to inside, glue a length of 5/8"w ribbon along spine
6. Follow Step 5 of Mantel Scarf, this page, to make frog; hot glue to journal.

"CHRISTMAS TEA" LAMP
(Shown on page 35)

You will need a silver teapot with lid (we used a 9 1/2"h x 10 1/2"w teapot); hacksaw; welding compound; drill with 3/8" dia. high-speed drill bit; 3/8" IP lamp parts from electrical supply store: five lock nuts, two 2" lengths of threaded pipe, harp cradle, socket base with shell, electrical cord with male plug on one end, and a lamp harp; seam ripper; scallop-edged lampshade to fit lamp; tissue paper; fabric to cover lampshade; spray adhesive; 1/2"w gimp trim; and a hot glue gun.

If your teapot lid does not have a knob, purchase a finial to fit lamp harp. Refer to Lamp Diagram, page 128, to assemble lamp.

1. Remove lid from teapot. Use hacksaw to remove knob from lid. Use welding compound to attach nut to bottom of knob for lamp finial.
2. Drill a hole through center top of lid and center bottom of pot; replace lid.
3. Place one 2" threaded pipe piece through hole at bottom of pot. Twist one lock nut onto pipe at bottom outside of pot until lock nut is flush with end of pipe; twist one lock nut onto pipe inside pot until tight against bottom of pot.
4. Place remaining pipe through hole in lid. Twist one lock nut 1" onto pipe inside lid; twist remaining lock nut onto pipe until tight against top of lid.
5. Twist harp cradle, then socket base, onto top of pipe until tight against lock nut. Loosen screws on socket shell. Thread electrical cord through pipe from bottom to lid. Wrap one wire on cord around one screw on socket shell twice; tighten screw. Repeat to attach remaining wire to opposite side. Snap socket shell into socket base.

Continued on page 128

6. Place ends of lamp harp into harp cradle.

7. Use seam ripper to carefully remove trim from lampshade; remove any threads from trim and set aside.

8. For lampshade pattern, center tissue paper over one section of shade and tape in place. Trace along edges of section; remove paper. Cut out shape along drawn lines.

9. For each section, position pattern on desired area of fabric; use a pencil to lightly draw around pattern. Cut out shape; use spray adhesive to attach fabric piece to lampshade.

10. Glue original trim to sides, then top of lampshade. Glue gimp trim along bottom edge of lampshade.

11. Place lampshade on harp; twist finial onto harp to secure lampshade.

LAMP DIAGRAM

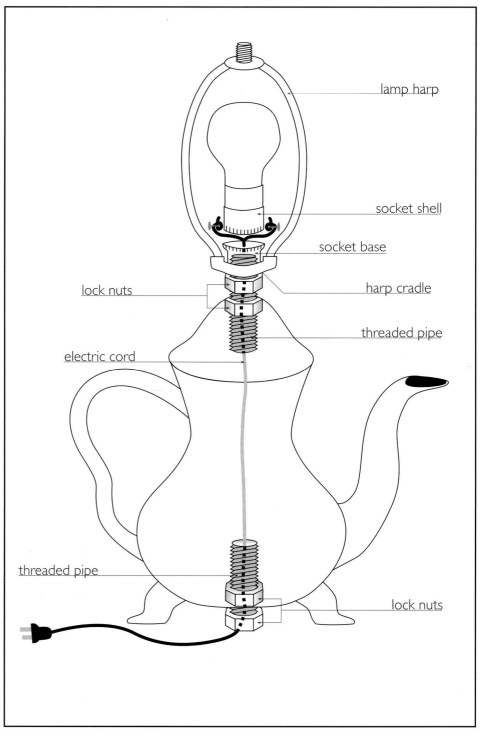

lamp harp

socket shell

socket base

lock nuts

harp cradle

threaded pipe

electric cord

threaded pipe

lock nuts

WOODLAND HAVEN

BIRDHOUSE ORNAMENTS
(Shown on page 40)

 You will need a utility knife; toilet paper tube for each small birdhouse or paper towel tube for each large birdhouse; white, ivory, and black acrylic paint; paintbrushes; crackle medium; utility scissors; medium-weight craft steel; hot glue gun; craft knife; push pin; ⁵/₈" long twigs for perches; tree bark for base; sheet moss; textured snow medium; and a toothbrush.

Allow paint, crackle medium, and snow medium to dry after each application.

1. Use utility knife to trim toilet paper tube to 4¹/₂" or paper towel tube to 7¹/₂". For birdhouse top, refer to Fig. I to cut one end of tube to a point.

Fig. I

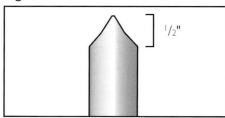

2. (*Note: Apply paint and crackle medium in one direction around tube to create a birchbark effect.*) Paint tube black. Apply one thick coat of crackle medium to tube. Apply an uneven coat of ivory paint to tube.
3. For roof, use utility scissors to cut a 2³/₈" × 4⁷/₈" piece from steel; bend steel in half. Glue roof to top of birdhouse.
4. For openings, use craft knife to make ¹/₂" dia. holes in birdhouse. Use point of push pin to make a hole for each perch just below each opening. Glue end of one twig in each hole.
5. Glue birdhouse on bark base. Arrange and glue moss on base. Apply snow medium along edges of roof and on base. Refer to *Spatter Painting*, page 156, to spatter paint roof with white paint.

WOODLAND ORNAMENTS
(Shown on page 39)

 For each ornament, you will need tracing paper; tissue paper; removable fabric marking pen; two 8" squares of felt (tan for acorn, ecru for bunny, and light teal for bird); straight pins; ecru, green, dark green, teal, dark teal, brown, and dark brown 3-ply Persian wool yarn; crewel embroidery needle; pearl and gold seed beads, beading thread, and a beading needle for bunny and bird ornaments; polyester fiberfill; and clear nylon thread.

Refer to Embroidery Stitches, page 156, and Stitching Key, page 130, for embroidery stitches, yarn colors, and bead placement before beginning project. Use one ply of yarn for all embroidery.

1. Trace desired embroidery design onto tissue paper. Center and pin tissue paper design on one felt square. Follow Stitching Key to work design on felt, filling in spaces with extra stitches as desired; carefully tear away paper. Use beading thread to add beads, if indicated.

2. Place felt squares together; cut out shapes 1" outside edge of design.
3. Matching right sides and leaving an opening for turning, use a ¹/₂" seam allowance to sew shapes together. Trim seam allowance to ¹/₄". Clip curves, turn right side out, and stuff with fiberfill; sew opening closed.
4. For hanger, thread 10" of clear thread through top of ornament. Knot thread ends together.

"A PEACEFUL CHRISTMASTIDE"
(Shown on page 40)

 Refer to Cross Stitch, page 157, before beginning project. Follow the chart and stitch key, page 131. Use three strands of floss for Cross Stitch, one strand for Half Cross Stitch, two strands for DMC #991 Backstitch, and one strand for all other backstitch.

Stitch design over two fabric threads on a 13" × 16" piece of Tea-Dyed Irish Linen (28 ct.). Our finished piece was custom framed.

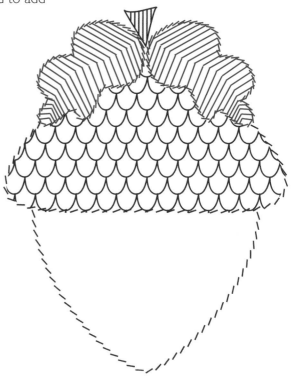

STITCHING KEY

Stitch Name	Symbol	Color
Lazy Daisy	⬭	light green
	⬬	dark brown
Five-petal Lazy Daisy	✺	dark teal
Stem Stitch	/////	ecru
	/////	teal
	/////	dark brown
	/////	light green
	/////	dark green
Satin Stitch	≡	dark green
	≡	dark brown
Feather Stitch	⩊⩊	dark brown
Straight Stitch	—	dark green
	—	light green
	—	dark brown
French Knot	●	dark brown
Bead	◎	white
	◍	gold

68w x 101h

X	DMC	¼ X	½X	B'ST
•	blanc	•		
O	ecru			
Π	353			
	356			∕
♥	434	∕		∕
⊟	435			
⊖	436			
+	437	∕		
⊙	523	∕		
	640		♥	
P	644	∕		
−	712			
$	738			
Σ	739			
▦	754	⦂		
X	758	∕		
∗	760	∕		
✔	761	∕		
	807		H	
V	822	∕		
	838			∕
T	951	∕		
	991			∕
★	3022	∕		
2	3023	∕		
◆	3033	∕		
■	3064	∕		
	3328			∕

131

WOODLAND GIFT BAGS
(Shown on page 39)

For each bag, you will need ecru felt for bunny or tan felt for acorn; tracing paper; tissue paper; fabric marking pen; ecru, green, dark green, teal, dark teal, brown, and dark brown 3-ply Persian wool yarn; crewel embroidery needle; pearl and gold seed beads and beading needle for bunny only; thread to match felt; polyester fiberfill; two 48" lengths of 1"w green ribbon for large bag; and 18" each of 1"w brown and ³⁄₈"w teal satin ribbon for small bag.

Refer to Embroidery Stitches, page 156 and Stitching Key, page 130, for embroidery stitches, yarn colors, and bead placement before beginning project. Use one ply of yarn for all embroidery.

1. Cut an 8" square from felt. Follow Step 1 of Woodland Ornaments, page 129, to embroider bunny for large bag or acorn for small bag on felt; cut out shape ¹⁄₄" outside edge of design.
2. Cut a 12¹⁄₂" × 28" piece of felt for large bag or a 6¹⁄₂" × 24" piece of felt for small bag. Center embroidered shape 7¹⁄₂" below one short edge on large bag piece or 5" below one short edge on small bag piece. Using narrow zigzag stitch, sew edges of embroidered felt shape to bag piece.
3. Cut a small opening in bag piece behind embroidered shape. Stuff shape with fiberfill; sew opening closed.
4. For large bag, cut two 1" × 12¹⁄₂" felt strips for casings. Pin strips 3¹⁄₂" from short edges on wrong side of bag piece. Sew along long edges of strips to secure.
5. (Note: Do not sew across casing ends on large bag.) Matching right sides and short edges and using a ¹⁄₄" seam allowance, sew sides of bag together.
6. For bottom of bags, flatten one corner to form point with side seam down center of point (Fig. 1). Sew across corner of bag 1" to 1¹⁄₂" from point; trim seam allowance to ¹⁄₄". Repeat for opposite corner. Turn bag right side out.

Fig. 1

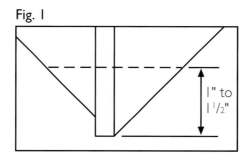

7. For large bag, refer to Fig. 2 to thread 48" ribbons through casings. Place gift in bag. Pull ribbons to gather bag and tie into a bow at both sides of bag. For small bag, use 18" ribbons to tie bag closed.

Fig. 2

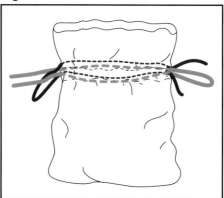

WOODLAND SANTA
(Shown on page 38)

You will need tacky wax, 17¹⁄₄" of ³⁄₄" dia. wooden dowel, 4¹⁄₄"h porcelain Santa head with chest and hands, polyester fiberfill, crib-size cotton batting, two 16" lengths of 16-gauge wire, hot glue gun, pliers, muslin, thread to match fabrics, heavy-duty thread, drill, 6" to 7" dia. ³⁄₄" thick wooden plaque, wood glue, sea green cold-water dye, tracing paper, pinking shears, pencil, ruler, light teal #5 pearl cotton, light green embroidery floss, crewel embroidery needle, brown felt for bag, ¹⁄₄ yd. faux fur, 18" of yarn to match felt for bag, large-eye needle, items for bag and pocket (we used miniature toys, painted wooden cutouts, and greenery with fruit), wooden craft picks, 18" long straight stick, and clear nylon thread.

Refer to Embroidery Stitches, page 156, and Santa Diagram, page 133, before beginning project. Use a ¹⁄₄" seam allowance for all sewing unless otherwise indicated. Use one strand of pearl cotton when working Blanket Stitches and two strands of floss when working Lazy Daisy Stitches. Use hot glue for all gluing unless otherwise indicated.

1. Apply wax to one end of dowel; insert firmly into head. Stuff head with fiberfill.
2. For arms, cut two 7" × 14" pieces from batting. Centering wire along one long edge, wrap each wire with one batting piece; glue edge of batting to secure. With one wire on each side of dowel, center arms under shoulders and glue in place. Use pliers to twist ends of wires together to secure.
3. With palms facing down, insert ends of arms into hands; stuff batting of arms into hands and glue to secure.
4. For body, sew long edges of an 11¹⁄₂" × 16" piece of muslin together to form tube; turn tube right side out. Baste around tube ¹⁄₄" from each end. With seam of tube centered at back, cut 3" long openings at each side of tube ³⁄₄" from top edge.
5. Place dowel in tube; insert arms through openings. Pull thread ends to gather top end of tube around neck; knot and trim ends. Stuff body with fiberfill; pull thread ends to tighten bottom of tube around dowel.
6. Drill a hole in center of plaque to fit dowel. Use wood glue to secure dowel in hole; allow to dry, propping as needed to hold dowel upright.
7. For coat and hat, follow manufacturer's instructions to dye a 12" × 32" piece of batting to desired shade. Matching long edges, fold batting in half. Refer to *Making Patterns*, page 154, to trace patterns, pages 134 – 139, onto tracing paper. Pinning patterns to fabric as indicated in Fig. 1 and cutting through both layers of batting, use pinking shears to cut two coat front pieces, one coat back piece, two sleeves, two pockets, and one hat piece from batting.

Fig. I

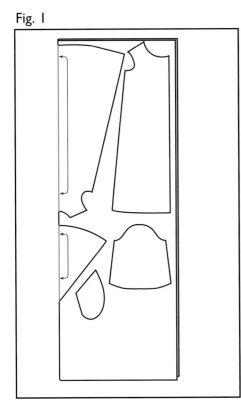

8. Stitch coat front and back pieces together at shoulder seams. For each sleeve, pin one sleeve to arm opening (Fig. 2); stitch in place.

Fig. 2

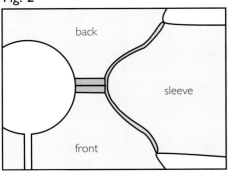

9. Stitch coat front and back together along sleeve and side seams (Fig. 3). Turn coat right side out; press.

Fig. 3

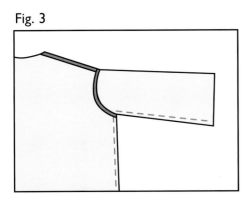

10. Matching straight edges, fold hat in half. Stitch straight edges together; turn right side out.

11. Use pencil and ruler to lightly mark placement for embroidery 1" from edge along one coat opening, bottom edges of coat and hat, and ¹/₂" from edges of sleeves.

12. Working *Blanket Stitches* along placement lines and *Lazy Daisy Stitches* between *Blanket Stitches*, embroider coat and hat. Pin pockets to coat. Stitching through both layers, work *Blanket Stitches* along side and bottom edges of pockets to secure, then work *Lazy Daisy Stitches* between *Blanket Stitches*.

13. Cutting through back of fur only, cut one 1" × 15" strip for coat opening, one 1" × 25" strip for bottom edge of coat, one ³/₄" × 10¹/₂" strip for hat; cut two ³/₄" × 7" strips for sleeves and two ¹/₂" × 3" strips for tops of pockets. Use collar pattern to cut collar from fur.

14. Glue fur strips along rim of hat, edges of sleeves, tops of pockets, bottom of coat, then opening of coat.

15. Place coat on Santa and overlap opening edges; tack closed along opening. For collar, use heavy-duty thread to work *Running Stitches* along short, straight edge; pull threads to gather collar to fit neck. Place collar on Santa and tack ends together to secure.

16. For bag, use pinking shears to cut a 7" × 12" piece and a ³/₄" × 12" strip from felt. Matching short edges, fold felt piece in half. Sew long edges of felt piece together; turn bag right side out. Tack ends of strip inside bag at seams. Using yarn and large-eye needle, work *Running Stitches* 1" from top edge of bag. Fill bag ²/₃ full with fiberfill. Glue craft picks to backs of small toys and cutouts as needed. Arrange items in bag and glue in place. Pull yarn ends to tighten bag around toys and tie into a bow; knot and trim ends. Place bag on Santa and arrange as desired. Place additional items in opposite pocket and glue in place.

17. Bend arms as desired. Wrapping and knotting thread around stick, hand, and wrist, use clear thread to secure stick to hand at desired height. Arrange hat on Santa; tack folds in place as desired.

SANTA DIAGRAM

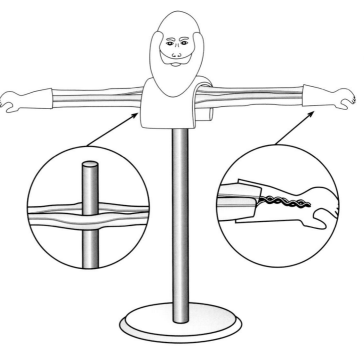

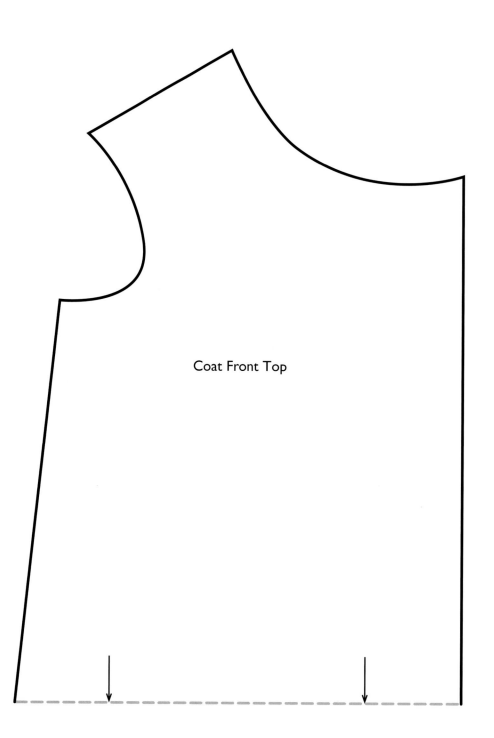

Coat Front Top

Coat Front Bottom

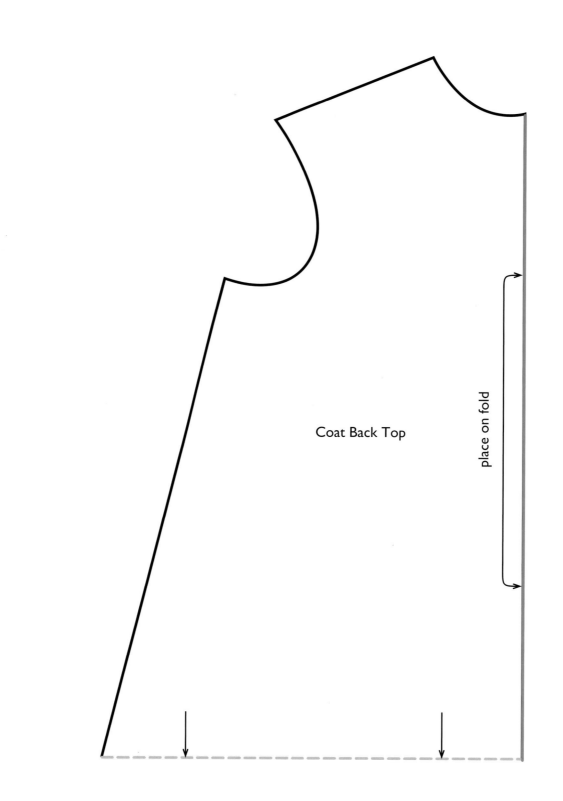

Coat Back Top

place on fold

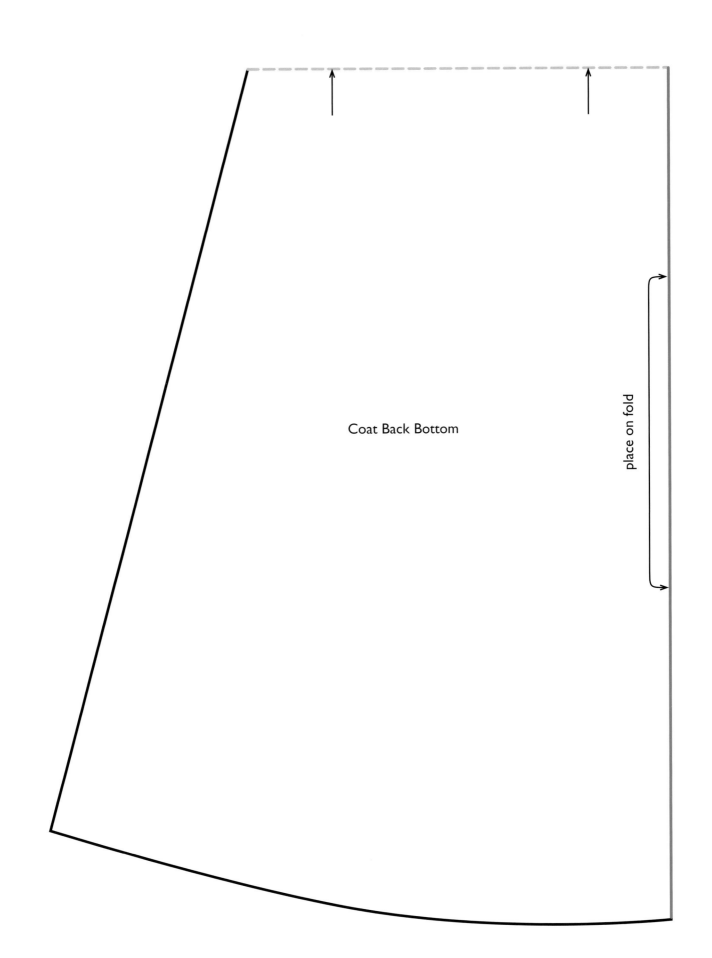

Coat Back Bottom

place on fold

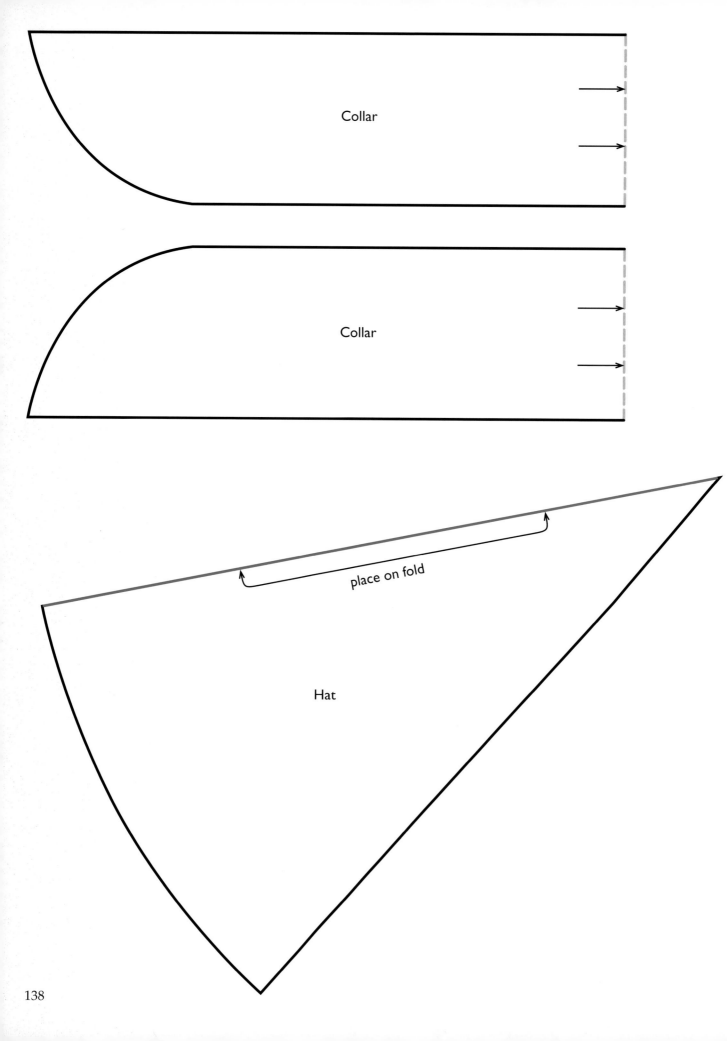

Collar

Collar

place on fold

Hat

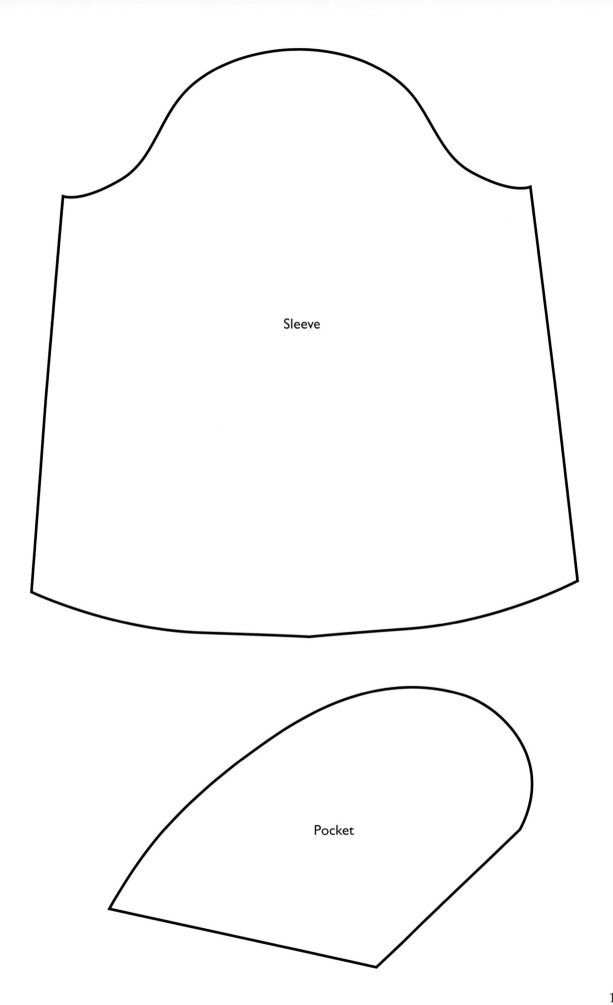

Sleeve

Pocket

PRIMITIVE GOLD STAR ORNAMENTS
(Shown on page 46)

For each ornament, you will need tracing paper, gold felt, dark red embroidery floss, $^7/_8$" dia. button, polyester fiberfill, pinking shears, and jute twine.

1. Trace small star pattern, page 146, onto tracing paper. Using pattern, cut two stars from felt.
2. Use floss to sew button at center of one star shape.
3. Matching wrong sides, place star shapes together. Using six strands of floss and leaving an opening for stuffing, work *Running Stitches*, page 157, along edges of star. Stuff star with fiberfill; sew opening closed. Use pinking shears to trim edges of stars.
4. For hanger, tack center of an 8" length of jute to back of ornament.

WHIMSICAL SIGN ORNAMENTS
(Shown on page 46)

You will need ecru card stock, decorative-edge craft scissors, red corrugated craft cardboard, hot glue gun, straight twigs, and miniature pinecones.

1. Photocopy sign designs, page 143, onto card stock. Use craft scissors to cut out designs.
2. For each sign, use regular scissors to cut a $3^1/_2$" × 6" piece from cardboard; cut points along ends.
3. Center and glue design to cardboard piece.
4. Glue $3^1/_2$", then 5" pieces of twigs along edges of design; glue a pinecone to each corner. Glue a 12" length of twig to back of sign.

FEED CONE ORNAMENTS
(Shown on page 46)

For each ornament, you will need a hot glue gun, 3" dia. plastic foam ball, $3^3/_{16}$" dia. × $6^1/_4$"h rusted cone ornament with hanger and star, craft glue, popping corn, one $3^1/_2$" square of fabric, 3" square of burlap, dark red embroidery floss, $^7/_8$" dia. button, decorative-edge craft scissors, photocopy of sign design (page 143) on ecru card stock, red corrugated craft cardboard, and a 6" long straight twig.

Allow craft glue to dry after each application. Use hot glue unless otherwise indicated.

1. Glue foam ball in cone. Cover top of ball with craft glue; dip and roll cone in corn, covering completely.
2. Press fabric square in half diagonally. Cut burlap square in half diagonally. Center burlap triangle on fabric triangle. Using six strands of floss, work *Running Stitches*, page 157, $^1/_4$" from edges of burlap to sew triangles together. Fray edges of burlap close to stitching. Sew button at center of triangles. Use craft glue to attach triangle to front of cone.
3. Use craft scissors to cut design from card stock. Use regular scissors to cut a $2^1/_8$" × $3^3/_4$" piece from cardboard; cut points in ends of cardboard. Center and glue design on cardboard piece.
4. Glue sign to twig. Removing corn kernel if necessary, insert end of sign into foam.

JOLLY REINDEER ORNAMENTS
(Shown on page 46)

For each ornament, you will need tracing paper, light brown plush felt, brown regular felt, craft glue, $^7/_8$" dia. button to cover, fabric to cover button, two $^3/_8$" dia. black shank buttons for eyes, brown and black embroidery floss, polyester fiberfill, rusty craft wire, wire cutters, and jute twine.

Allow glue to dry after each application.

1. Trace head, ear, and inner ear patterns, page 146, onto tracing paper. Using patterns, cut two heads (one in reverse) and two ears from plush felt. Cut two inner ears from brown felt.
2. For each ear, glue one inner ear piece to wrong side of plush ear piece. Pinch bottom of ear to form pleat; glue to secure.
3. For nose, follow manufacturer's instructions to cover button with fabric. Sew eyes and nose to right side of one head shape. Using six strands of black floss, work three *Running Stitches*, page 157, vertically below nose. Arrange and tack ears on wrong side of same head shape.
4. Matching wrong sides, place head shapes together. Using six strands of brown floss and leaving an opening for stuffing, work *Running Stitches* along edge of head. Stuff head with fiberfill; sew opening closed.
5. For each antler, cut three 4" lengths of wire; twist together at one end. Apply glue to twisted ends and insert into top of head between layers of felt; allow to dry. Bend and trim antlers as desired.
6. For hanger, tack center of an 8" length of jute to back of ornament.

FRIENDLY POSABLE DEER TOPPER

(Shown on page 44)

You will need tracing paper; light brown plush felt; gold, brown, and black regular felt; pinking shears; 18-gauge wire; wire cutters; polyester fiberfill; one Jolly Reindeer Ornament (without hanger); dark red embroidery floss; 7/8" dia. button; 14" of 1"w ribbon; and a 1 1/8" dia. rusted bell.

Use a 1/4" seam allowance for all sewing unless otherwise indicated. Refer to Embroidery Stitches, page 156, before beginning project. Use six strands of floss for all embroidery.

1. Referring to Assembly Diagram, page 144, trace a whole body pattern onto tracing paper. Trace tail, large star, and hoof patterns, pages 146 and 147, onto tracing paper. Using patterns, cut two bodies and two tails from plush felt and eight hooves from black felt; use pinking shears to cut two stars from gold felt.
2. Matching right sides, place body pieces together. Refer to Fig. 1 to sew body pieces together along blue lines; turn right side out.
3. Using traced body pattern as a guide, bend wire to shape reindeer form. Place wire form in body. Lightly stuff legs with fiberfill; firmly stuff body.
4. For each hoof, fold hoof piece in half, matching short ends; sew along side edges and turn right side out. Leaving an opening for stuffing, sew hoof to one leg. Stuff with fiberfill and sew opening closed. For indention in hoof, make a stitch through center and around bottom of hoof.
5. Sew edges of neck together, then lightly stuff with fiberfill. Turn edge of neck 1/4" to wrong side and sew head to neck.
6. Matching wrong sides, sew tail pieces together; tack tail in place.
7. Using six strands of red floss and leaving an opening for stuffing, work two rows of *Running Stitches* along edges of stars to sew pieces together. Lightly stuff star with fiberfill and sew

opening closed. Sew button at center of star, then sew star to one hoof.
8. Thread bell onto ribbon; knot ribbon around neck and trim ends.

"EN-DEER-ING" TREE SKIRT

(Shown on page 44)

You will need 3 yds. of quilted muslin; string; fabric marking pencil; thumbtack; template plastic; craft knife and cutting mat; 1 1/2" yds. of fabric for prairie points, binding, pinked squares, and reindeer noses; tracing paper; light brown plush felt; brown regular felt; craft glue; covered button kit with eight 7/8" dia. buttons; sixteen 3/8" dia. black shank buttons for eyes; brown and black embroidery floss; and polyester fiberfill.

Use a 1/4" seam allowance for all sewing unless otherwise indicated. Refer to Embroidery Stitches, page 156, before beginning project. Use six strands of floss for all embroidery.

1. Matching short edges, fold muslin in half; cut along fold. Matching short edges, fold each piece in half.
2. Tie one end of string to fabric marking pencil. Insert thumbtack through string 27" from pencil. Refer to Fig. 1 to insert thumbtack in corner of one fabric piece and mark outer cutting line. Repeat for remaining fabric piece.

Fig. 1

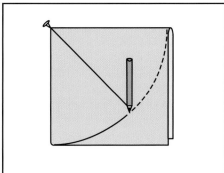

3. Repeat Step 2, inserting thumbtack 2" from the pencil to mark the inner cutting line. Cut along drawn lines through all layers of fabric.
4. Sew straight edges of pieces together. Matching seams, fold tree skirt in half; cut along one fold from outer edge to inner edge for opening of tree skirt.
5. Cut a 23" square from fabric. Follow *Making a Continuous Bias Strip*, page 154, to make a 1 1/4"w strip from fabric.
6. For binding, cut one 65" piece from bias strip. Press one long edge 3/8" to wrong side. Matching right sides and raw edges, sew strip along opening of skirt. Covering stitching, fold pressed edge to wrong side of skirt and pin in place. Sewing in seam on right side, sew binding to tree skirt.
7. For prairie points, trace Pattern A, page 144, onto template plastic; cut out. Use template to cut 49 squares from fabric. Matching wrong sides, press each square in half diagonally; press in half again (Fig. 2).

Fig. 2

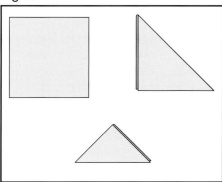

8. Cut two 5-yard lengths from bias strip. Press one long edge of each length 1/4" to wrong side. Overlap folded edge of two prairie points 1". Beginning at center and matching right sides and raw edges, pin prairie points to one strip (Fig. 3).

Fig. 3

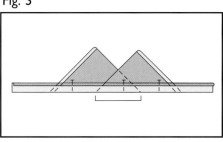

141

9. Insert folded edge of third prairie point 1" between open edges of one prairie point (Fig. 4). Repeat for remaining prairie points along each edge of strip; baste in place.

Fig. 4

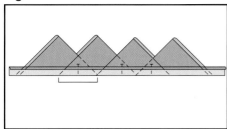

10. Matching raw edges and prairie point side of strip to right side of remaining strip, sew strips together along raw edge. Press strips toward each other to form binding.

11. Beginning with center of strip at center on edge of tree skirt, insert edge of skirt into binding; pin in place. Cut binding ends 1" past opening edges. Fold 1/2" to wrong side, then fold to back of tree skirt; pin in place. Top stitch along top and bottom edges of binding.

12. Trace head, ear, and inner ear patterns, page 146, onto tracing paper. For each reindeer head, use patterns to cut one head and two ears from plush felt and two inner ears from brown felt; cut out eight reindeer total.

13. For each ear, glue one inner ear piece to wrong side of plush ear piece. Pinch bottom of ear to form pleat; glue to secure.

14. For nose, follow manufacturer's instructions to cover one button with fabric. Sew eyes and nose to right side of head shape. Using black floss, work three *Running Stitches* vertically below nose. Arrange and tack ears on wrong side of head shape.

15. Cut seven 3" squares from burlap. Pull several threads on each burlap square to fray edges. Use pinking shears to cut seven 4" squares from red fabric. For each patch, center a burlap square on a red square. Sew a button at center of squares.

16. Arrange and pin reindeer heads and layered squares around edge of tree skirt. Leaving an opening for stuffing, use brown floss to work *Running Stitches* along edges of each head. Stuff heads with fiberfill and sew openings closed. Use brown floss to work *Running Stitches* along edges of each burlap square.

17. Use brown floss to work *Stem Stitches* for antlers.

HOMESPUN STOCKINGS
(Shown on page 45)

STOCKING WITH PATCHES

 You will need one 20" x 24" piece of plush felt for stocking front and back, brown floss, 5" x 9" piece of quilted muslin for cuff, 2 1/4" x 8" fabric piece for hanger, scraps of fabric and burlap for patches, and four 7/8" dia. buttons.

Use a 1/4" seam allowance for all sewing unless otherwise indicated. Use six strands of floss for all Running Stitches.

1. For pattern, enlarge stocking pattern, page 115, 160% on copier; cut out pattern.

2. Matching short edges, fold muslin piece in half; use pattern to cut two stocking pieces from muslin.

3. For patches, cut three 2" squares from fabric and two 2" squares from burlap; fray edges of burlap squares 1/4". Arrange and pin one fabric and one burlap patch on toe of stocking front; work *Running Stitches*, page 157, along edges of patches. Use floss to sew one 7/8" dia. button to center of burlap patch. Leaving top edge unstitched, work *Running Stitches* 3/8" from edges of stocking front.

4. For cuff cut a 3" x 7 1/2" piece from muslin; trim edges to match top of stocking. Work *Running Stitches* 1/4" from edges of cuff. Arrange and pin patches on cuff; work *Running Stitches* along edges of patches. . Use floss to sew one 7/8" dia. button to center of each patch. Sew cuff to stocking front.

5. Matching wrong sides, place stocking front on stocking back; leaving top edge open, sew pieces together.

6. For hanger, press fabric strip in half lengthwise; unfold strip. Press long edges of strip to center; refold. Topstitch along each long edge. Fold strip in half to form a loop; tack ends inside stocking at heelside seam.

REINDEER STOCKING

 You will need a 20" x 24" piece of quilted muslin for stocking front and back, fabric and burlap scraps for patches, one 7/8" dia. button, tracing paper, light brown plush felt, brown regular felt, craft glue, one 7/8" dia. button to cover, fabric to cover button, two 3/8" dia. black shank buttons for eyes, brown and black embroidery floss, polyester fiberfill, template plastic, craft knife and cutting mat, 1/2 yd. of fabric for prairie points and binding, 2" x 8" fabric piece for hanger, rusty craft wire, and wire cutters.

Use a 1/4" seam allowance for all sewing unless otherwise indicated. Refer to Embroidery Stitches, page 156, before beginning project. Use six strands of floss for all embroidery.

1. For pattern, enlarge stocking pattern page 115, 160% on copier; cut out pattern.

2. Matching short edges, fold felt piece in half; use pattern to cut two stocking pieces from felt.

3. For toe patches, cut one 2" square each from fabric and burlap; fray edges of burlap squares 1/4". Arrange and pin patches on toe of stocking front. Use brown floss to work *Running Stitches* along edges of patches and to sew 7/8" dia. button to center of burlap patch. Leaving top edge unstitched, use brown floss to work *Running Stitches* 3/8" from edges of stocking front.

4. Follow Steps 12 – 14 of "En-Deer-ing" Tree Skirt to make reindeer head. Arrange and pin reindeer head on stocking. Leaving an opening for stuffing, work *Running Stitches* along edges of head. Stuff head with fiberfill and sew opening closed; work three *Cross Stitches* on stocking front.

5. Matching wrong sides, place stocking front on stocking back; leaving top edge open, sew pieces together.

6. Using Pattern A, page 144, follow Step 7 of "En-Deer-ing" Tree Skirt to make prairie points. Matching raw edges of points to top edge of stocking and beginning at center front of stocking, arrange and pin points along edge of stocking.

7. Cut a 1¹⁄₂"w x 15" bias strip from fabric. Press one long edge of strip ¹⁄₄" to wrong side; press one end of strip ¹⁄₄" to wrong side.

8. Matching raw edges and beginning with pressed end at center back of stocking, sew strip to stocking. Fold strip over top edge and stitch in place.

9. For hanger, press fabric strip in half lengthwise; unfold strip. Press long edges of strip to center; refold. Topstitch along each long edge. Fold strip in half to form a loop; tack ends inside stocking at heelside seam.

10. For each antler, cut three 4" lengths of wire; twist together at one end. Apply glue to twisted ends and insert into top of head between layers of felt; allow to dry. Bend and trim antlers as desired.

Leg

ASSEMBLY DIAGRAM

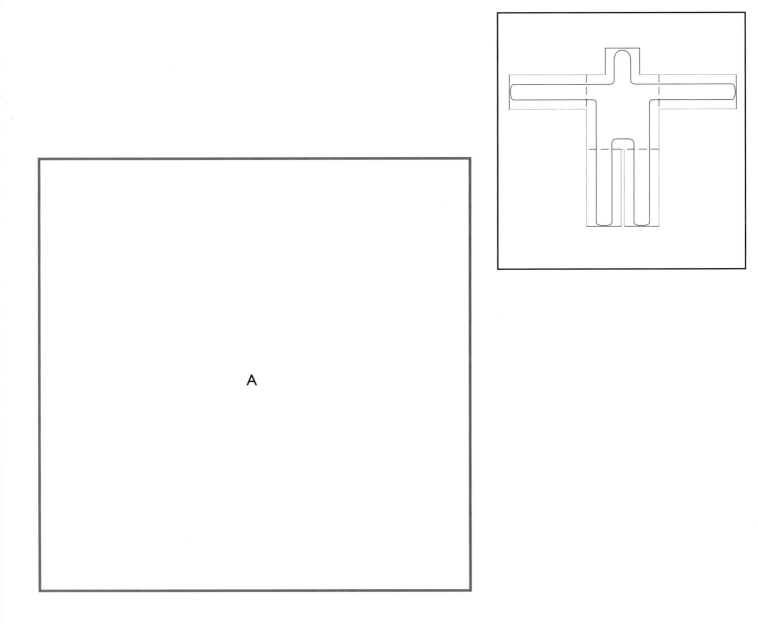

A

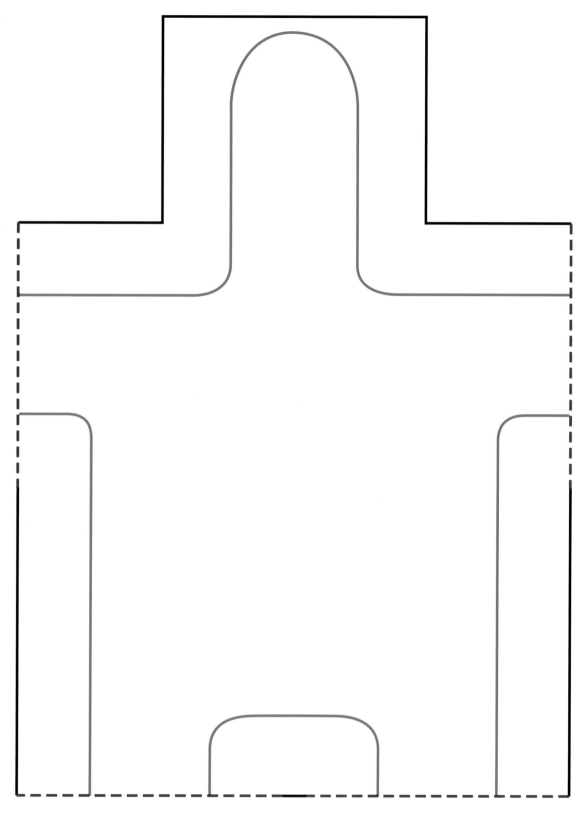

Body

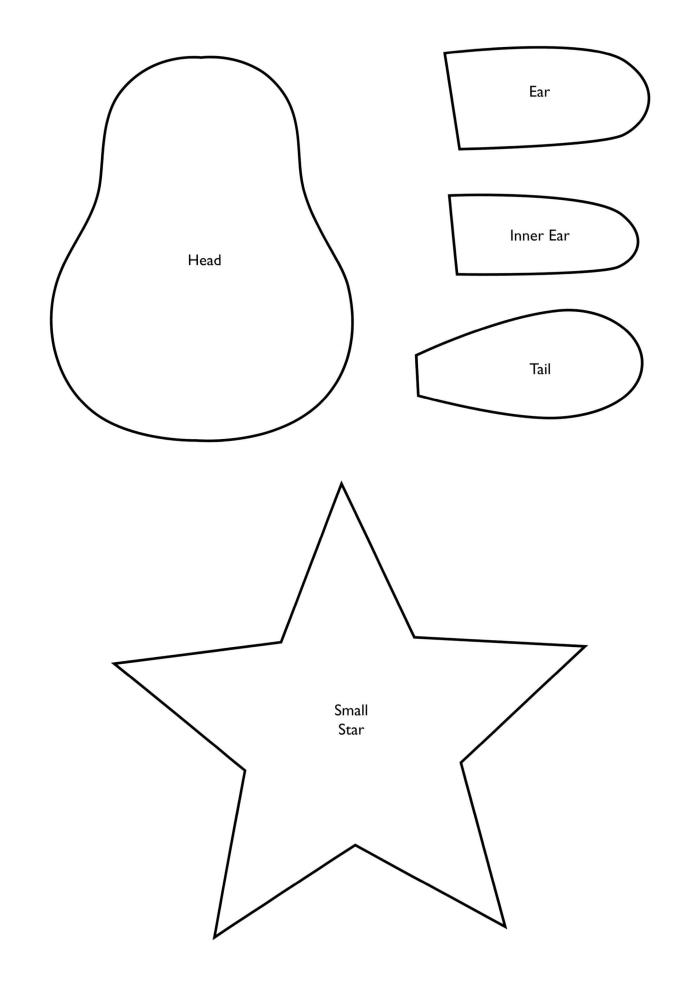

Head

Ear

Inner Ear

Tail

Small
Star

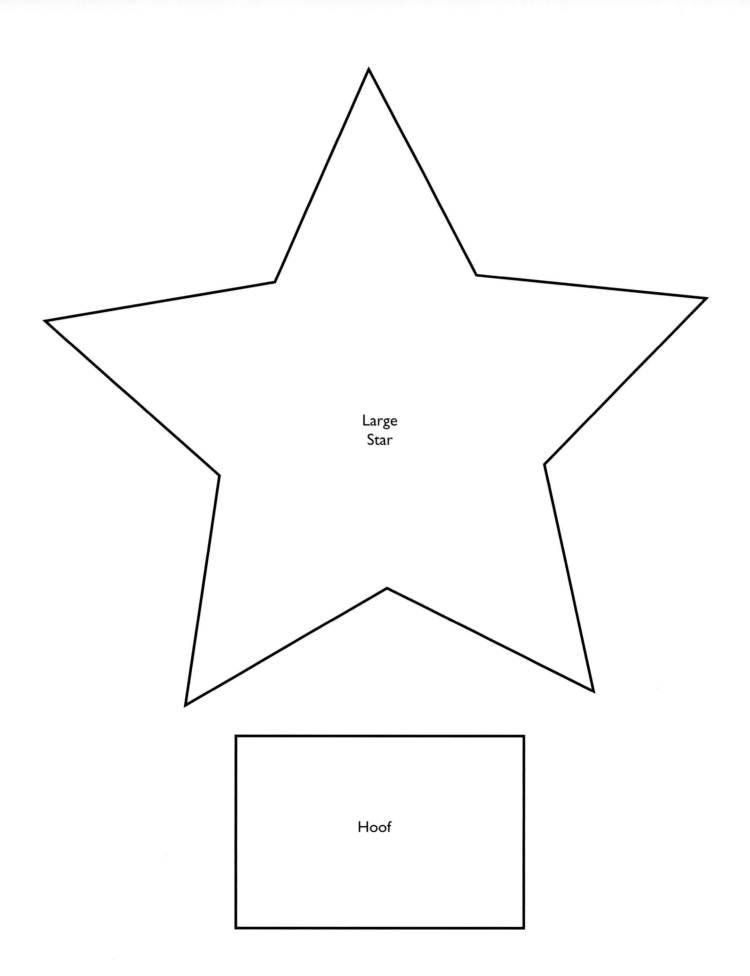

Large
Star

Hoof

DECORATING MADE EASY

ADVENT BASKET
(Shown on page 51)

 You will need a basket with flat back to hang on wall, artificial pine garland, hot glue gun, rusted craft wire, 1/2" dia. dowel, small twigs, 3" long cinnamon sticks, natural raffia, and dried pepper berries and oranges.

1. Arrange a length of garland along front rim of basket; glue to secure.
2. Measure along front rim of basket over garland; multiply measurement by 2. Cut two lengths of craft wire the determined measurement. Twist wires together at each end, then wrap wires around dowel to curl. Stretch curled wires to fit along rim of basket, tuck into garland, and glue to secure.
3. For cinnamon stick bundles, knot several lengths of raffia around two or three cinnamon sticks.
4. Arrange and glue cinnamon stick bundles, clusters of pepper berries, oranges, and small bunches of twigs to garland as desired.

ADVENT BOXES
(Shown on page 51)

 You will need an awl, twenty-four small papier-mâché boxes with rusted tin lids (we used 2 1/4" square and 2 1/4" dia. round boxes), jute twine, and a white paint pen.

1. For each box, use awl to punch a hole in side of box.
2. For hanger, knot ends of a 6" length of jute together to form a loop. Thread loop end of hanger up through hole until knot catches on inside of box.
3. Use paint pen to write "Love", "Hope", "Joy", or "Peace" on lid; allow to dry.

ADVENT SIGN
(Shown on page 51)

 You will need a 8 1/2" x 11" piece of handmade paper, spray adhesive, decorative-edge craft scissors, 8 1/2" x 11" piece of corrugated craft cardboard, cinnamon sticks, natural raffia, 7 1/2" x 10" piece of cardboard, and dried pepper berries.

Use hot glue for all gluing unless otherwise indicated.

1. Photocopy Advent sign, facing page, onto handmade paper; cut out just inside border. Apply spray adhesive to wrong side of sign. Center and smooth sign on corrugated side of craft cardboard. Use craft scissors to trim edges of craft cardboard.
2. Cut lengths of cinnamon sticks to fit along edges of sign; glue in place.
3. For hanger, knot three 12" lengths of raffia together at center; glue ends to top edge on back of sign.
4. Center and glue cardboard piece on back of sign.
5. Glue clusters of leaves and berries at corners and top center of cinnamon stick border.

CLASSIC CHRISTMAS CENTERPIECE
(Shown on page 53)

 You will need an 8 1/2" dia. x 1" thick flat foam wreath; gold Design Master® floral spray; 1 1/2"w sheer gold, 2 3/8"w gold net, and 3 1/2"w sheer red wire-edged ribbons; 4" long wired floral picks; garden clippers; organza to puddle under centerpiece; a large pillar candle to fit in opening of wreath; fresh evergreen sprigs; and ornaments.

1. Spray wreath with gold paint; allow to dry.
2. Cut six 16" lengths from each width of ribbon. For each ribbon loop, match ends of one ribbon length and gather around wired end of floral pick (Fig. 1); wrap wire around gathers to secure.

Fig. 1

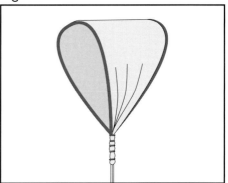

3. Cut two 36" lengths from each width of ribbon. For each streamer, gather one end of streamer around wired end of floral pick; wrap wire around gathers to secure.
4. Trimming floral picks as necessary, arrange loops on wreath to drape over top and edges. Insert one of each width streamer on opposite sides of wreath; notch streamer ends to desired lengths.
5. Arrange organza on table. Place wreath on organza and candle in wreath; tuck ornaments and sprigs of evergreen among loops and streamers.

Advent

the season of

Love·Hope·Joy & Peace

THE SHARING OF CHRISTMAS

GARDENER'S WINDOW BOX

(Shown on page 58)

You will need tracing paper; compressed craft sponge; sharp scissors; artificial leaf; wooden planter; foam kneeling pad; white, yellow, purple, and green acrylic paint; paper towels, foam brush, and a small stencil brush.

Allow paint to dry after each application.

1. Trace flower design onto tracing paper; cut out. Draw around pattern onto sponge; cut out.
2. To "stamp" flowers onto kneeling pad, lightly dampen sponge piece. Dip sponge piece into paint and blot on paper towel to remove excess paint. Press sponge shape onto surface. Reapply paint to sponge as necessary.
3. To "stamp" leaves onto planter and kneeling pad, dip sponge brush into paint and blot on a paper towel to remove excess paint. Brush leaf with paint, then press leaf onto surface. Reapply paint to leaf as necessary.
4. Use stencil brush to paint flower center.

DOG LOVER'S GIFT COLLECTION

(Shown on page 60)

SUPER SIMPLE DOG BED

You will need 1 yd. of 60"w flannel, 33" of ³/₄"w self-adhesive hook and loop fastener, two 28" x 34" pieces of muslin for cushion, and polyester fiberfill.

1. For cover, press short edges of flannel 1" to wrong side. Press 1" to wrong side again for hem; stitch in place. Center and adhere one side of hook and loop fastener along one hem on right side of fabric. Center and adhere remaining side of fastener along opposite hem on wrong side of fabric; fasten edges together.
2. Turn cover wrong side out. Place cover on a flat surface with fastened edges at center back; pin edges together to secure. Using a plate or other round object as a guide, draw round corners on cover; cut corners along drawn lines through both layers of fabric.
3. Using a ¹/₂" seam allowance, sew raw edges together; clip curves and turn cover right side out.
4. Leaving an opening for turning, use a ¹/₄" seam allowance to sew muslin pieces together; clip corners and turn right side out. Stuff cushion with fiberfill and sew opening closed. Place cushion in cover.

BEST FRIEND'S FRAME

You will need tracing paper, white craft foam, scissors or a craft knife and cutting mat, red paint pen, black permanent fine-point marker, craft glue, and a frame with a border that is at least 1¹/₂" wide (we used a 6" x 6" handmade paper-covered frame with decorative screws).

1. Trace bone pattern onto tracing paper; cut out. Draw around pattern on craft foam to make desired number of bones. Cut out shapes.
2. Use paint pen to write phrases and pet's name on bones; allow to dry. Outline letters with marker.
3. Glue bones to frame and allow to dry.

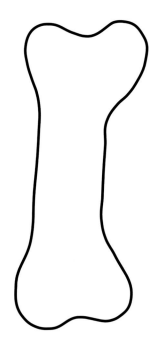

FESTIVE FLORAL TOPPER
(Shown on page 61)

You will need a glass jar, 3" thick plastic foam block, artificial holly leaves with berries, 18" lengths of floral wire, artificial holly picks, artificial poinsettia stems, green floral tape, cinnamon candies, hot glue gun, green floral foil, and two 2"w coordinating sheer ribbons.

1. Cut a piece of foam to fit in opening of jar; cover foam with foil and insert into neck of jar.
2. For candy flowers, glue one end of the wrapper on a piece of candy around one end of a piece of floral wire; wrap entire wire "stem" with floral tape. Adding holly leaves and catching leaf stems under tape, wrap stem with floral tape again.
3. Arrange candy flowers, holly picks, and poinsettias in foam.
4. Knot ribbons around neck of jar. Tie one ribbon into a bow; notch ribbon ends.

BEAD-EMBELLISHED BOX
(Shown on page 62)

You will need a 7¹/₂" dia. x 3"h papier-mâché box, batting, satin fabric, spray adhesive, 1" dia. covered button kit, awl, hot glue gun, beaded trim, gimp, beaded tassel, and felt to coordinate with satin fabric.

1. Draw around lid on batting and wrong side of fabric. Cut out batting along drawn line and fabric ¹/₂" outside drawn line.

2. Apply spray adhesive to one side of batting, smooth batting onto lid. Make clips in edge of fabric to ¹/₈" from drawn line. Apply spray adhesive to wrong side of fabric circle; center lid on wrong side of circle. Pulling fabric taut, glue clipped edges to side of lid.
3. Measure around lid, measure height of lid; cut a piece of poster board the determined measurements. Draw around poster board on wrong side of fabric; cut out ¹/₄" outside drawn line. Apply spray adhesive to wrong side of fabric; center and smooth poster board on fabric. Clipping corners of fabric as necessary, smooth fabric over edges of poster board. Glue strip around lid.
4. Follow manufacturer's instructions to cover button with fabric. Use awl to poke a small hole at center of lid; poke shank of button through hole. Hot glue shank on bottom of lid to secure. Overlapping ends, hot glue beaded trim, then gimp around side of lid. Hang tassel from button.
5. Measure around box; add ¹/₂". Measure height of box; add 1". Cut a strip from fabric the determined measurements. Draw a line ¹/₂" inside each long edge on wrong side of strip. Press one end ¹/₄" to wrong side. Make clips in edges of strip to ¹/₈" from drawn lines. Apply spray adhesive to wrong side of strip. Centering box between lines and overlapping pressed end over raw end, smooth strip around box. Smooth clipped edges to bottom and inside of box. Overlapping ends, hot glue gimp over clipped edge on inside of box.
6. Draw around box on felt; cut out ¹/₄" inside drawn line. Apply spray adhesive to wrong side of felt; smooth felt over bottom of box.

ETCHED GLASSES
(Shown on page 65)

For each glass, you will need clear contact paper, tracing paper, small sharp scissors or a craft knife and cutting mat, wine glass (we used glasses with a golden-yellow tint), etching cream, and 1"w wire-edged ribbon.

Follow etching cream manufacturer's instructions to clean glass before etching.

1. For each snowflake, cut a 2¹/₂" square from contact paper. Trace large or small snowflake pattern at center on paper side of square.
2. Cut snowflake from square; adhere square to glass. Cut center piece from snowflake; adhere center piece to glass at center of square. Make sure all edges of contact paper are adhered firmly to glass. Repeat with additional snowflakes as desired.
4. Follow manufacturer's instructions to apply etching cream to glass within edges of snowflake only.
5. Tie ribbon bows around stems of glasses; notch ribbon ends.

PAPER SILHOUETTES

(Shown on page 64)

 For each silhouette, you will need a portrait photograph, repositionable spray adhesive, black silhouette paper, small sharp scissors or craft knife and cutting mat, medium to heavy-weight decorative paper for background cut to fit in frame, and a frame with glass and backing.

Refer to Photography Tips and Silhouette Tips, this page, before beginning project.

1. Take several profile pictures of your subject. Select photo. Photos can be sized and reversed using a photocopier or computer with a scanner; size photo to fit in frame.
2. Apply adhesive to the back of copy and smooth onto white side of silhouette paper.
3. Carefully cut out silhouette; cut a curved line across bottom. Remove photocopy image.
4. Apply spray adhesive to back of silhouette. Arrange and smooth silhouette onto background paper.
5. Mount silhouette in frame.

SILHOUETTE TIPS

Photography Tips

Turn subject sideways for a clear profile. Use a simple background for a sharp image, such as hanging a white sheet on a wall. It is best to have the light coming from behind subject, so that subject will be very dark and background will be light. If shooting inside, place a lamp behind subject, shining it onto the wall.

To eliminate shadows behind subject, position subject about 4- to 5-feet in front of a wall. Do not use a flash when shooting, or subject will be too light. To make sure photo isn't blurred, steady camera by mounting it on a tripod.

Try several different poses so there will be a good selection of photographs from which to choose. The finished silhouette will be in reverse from the original photo; either reverse subject's pose or reverse the photo on a photocopier or computer.

Silhouette Tips

If there are details on your silhouette that are too hard to cut out accurately, use a black permanent pen to draw in the details on background paper after silhouette is glued down.

Any details in a photo that do not translate well to your silhouette, for instance a bow in a child's hair, can be taken off when you cut out your silhouette.

DECOUPAGED CLOCK

(Shown on page 63)

 You will need an 11¹/₂" dia. wooden plate, light green and gold acrylic paint, color photocopy of clock design (facing page), spray adhesive, drill and drill bit required for clock kit, clock kit with pendulum, rub-on numbers, old tooth brush, wood-tone spray, and steel wool.

Allow paint, wood-tone spray, paint pen, decoupage glue, and sealer to dry after each application.

1. Paint plate green. Cut out copy of clock face design. Apply spray adhesive to wrong side of design; center and smooth design on back of plate. Follow manufacturer's instructions to drill a hole for clock kit at center of plate.
2. Use gold paint pen to draw over minute marks and inner and outer circles on clock face design. Apply numbers to green band around clock face design at corresponding minute marks.
3. Follow *Spatter Painting*, page 156, to lightly spatter clock face with gold acrylic paint. Lightly spray clock with wood-tone spray. Use steel wool to gently rub clock to distress paint.
4. Follow manufacturer's instructions to assemble clock kit.

153

GENERAL INSTRUCTIONS

MAKING PATTERNS

When entire pattern is shown, place tracing paper over pattern and trace pattern. For a more durable pattern, use a permanent marker to trace pattern onto stencil plastic.

When pattern pieces are stacked or overlapped, place tracing paper over pattern and follow a single color to trace pattern. Repeat to trace each pattern separately onto tracing paper.

When tracing a two-part pattern, match dashed lines and arrows to trace the pattern onto tracing paper.

When only half of pattern is shown (indicated by a solid blue line on pattern), fold tracing paper in half. Place the fold along solid blue line and trace pattern half. Place fold of pattern along fold in fabric.

SEWING SHAPES

1. Center pattern on wrong side of one fabric piece and use fabric marking pen to draw around pattern. Do not cut out shape.
2. Place fabric pieces right sides together. Leaving an opening for turning, carefully sew pieces together directly on drawn line.
3. Leaving a 1/4" seam allowance, cut out shape. Clip seam allowance at curves and corners. Turn right side out and press.

CUTTING A FABRIC CIRCLE

1. Cut a square of fabric the size indicated in project instructions.
2. Matching right sides, fold fabric square in half from top to bottom and again from left to right.

3. Tie one end of string to a pencil or fabric marking pen. Measuring from pencil, insert a thumbtack through string at length indicated in project instructions. Insert thumbtack through folded corner of fabric. Holding tack in place and keeping string taut, mark cutting line (Fig. 1).

Fig. 1

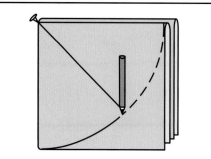

4. Cut along drawn line through all fabric layers.

FUSIBLE APPLIQUÉS

To prevent darker fabrics from showing through, white or light-colored fabrics may need to be lined with fusible interfacing before applying paper-backed fusible web.

To make reverse appliqué pieces, trace pattern onto tracing paper; turn traced paper over and continue to follow all steps using reversed pattern.

1. Use a pencil to trace pattern onto paper side of web as many times as indicated for each fabric. Repeat for additional patterns and fabrics.
2. Follow manufacturer's instructions to fuse traced patterns to wrong side of fabrics. Do not remove paper backing.
3. Cut out appliqués along traced lines. Remove paper backing.
4. Arrange appliqués, web side down, on project, overlapping as necessary. Appliqués can be temporarily held in place by touching appliqués with tip of iron. If appliqués are not in desired position, lift and reposition.
5. Fuse appliqués in place.

MACHINE APPLIQUÉ

1. Place paper or stabilizer on wrong side of background fabric under fused appliqué.
2. Beginning on a straight edge of appliqué if possible, position project under presser foot so that most of stitching will be on appliqué. Take a stitch in fabric and bring bobbin thread to top. Hold both threads toward you and sew over them for several stitches to secure; clip threads. Using a medium-width zigzag stitch, stitch over all exposed raw edges of appliqué(s) and along detail lines as indicated in instructions.
3. When stitching is complete, remove stabilizer. Clip threads close to stitching.

MAKING A CONTINUOUS BIAS STRIP

1. Cut a square from binding fabric the size indicated in the project instructions. Cut square in half diagonally to make two triangles.
2. With right sides together and using a 1/4" seam allowance, sew triangles together (Fig. 1); press seam allowance open.

Fig. 1

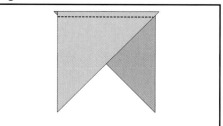

3. On wrong side of fabric, draw lines the width of the binding as specified in the project instructions, usually 2¹/₂" (Fig. 2). Cut off any remaining fabric less than this width.

Fig. 2

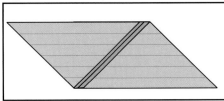

4. With right sides inside, bring short edges together to form a tube; match raw edges so that first drawn line of top section meets second drawn line of bottom section (Fig. 3).

Fig. 3

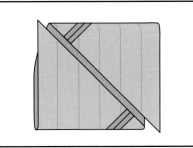

5. Carefully pin edges together by inserting pins through drawn lines at point where drawn lines intersect, making sure the pins go through intersections on both sides. Using a ¹/₄" seam allowance, sew edges together. Press seam allowance open.
6. To cut continuous strip, begin cutting along first drawn line (Fig. 4). Continue cutting along drawn line around tube.

Fig. 4

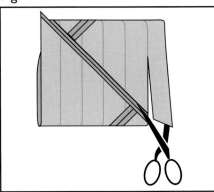

COFFEE OR TEA DYEING

Coffee Dyeing: Dissolve 2 tablespoons instant coffee in 2 cups hot water; allow to cool.
Tea Dyeing: Steep 1 tea bag in 2 cups hot water; remove bag and allow to cool.
For Both: Immerse fabric into coffee or tea. Soak until desired color is achieved. Remove fabric, rinse, and allow to dry; press if needed.

BOWS

Note: Loop sizes given in project instructions refer to the length of ribbon used to make one loop of bow. If no size is given, make loops desired size for project.

1. For first streamer, measure desired length of streamer from one end of ribbon; twist ribbon between fingers (Fig. 1).

Fig. 1

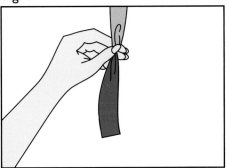

2. Keeping right side of ribbon facing out, fold ribbon to front to form desired-size loop; gather ribbon between fingers (Fig. 2). Fold ribbon to back to form another loop; gather ribbon between fingers (Fig. 3).

Fig. 2

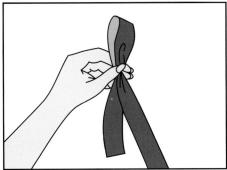

Fig. 3

3. (*Note:* If a center loop is desired, form half the desired number of loops, then loosely wrap ribbon around thumb and gather ribbon between fingers as shown in Fig. 4; form remaining loops.) Continue to form loops, varying size of loops as desired, until bow is desired size.

Fig. 4

4. For remaining streamer, trim ribbon to desired length.
5. To secure bow, hold gathered loops tightly. Fold a length of floral wire around gathers of loops. Hold wire ends behind bow, gathering all loops forward; twist bow to tighten wire. Arrange loops and trim ribbon ends as desired.

PAINTING TECHNIQUES

Preparing Project for Painting:
Remove any hardware and set aside. Repair any problems, such as holes, cracks, and other imperfections, as desired. Sand item and wipe with tack cloth. Apply primer and allow to dry. Paint project according to instructions. Clean hardware and replace, or replace with new hardware.

Tips for Painting on Fabric:
If painting on a garment, wash, dry, and press garment according to paint manufacturer's recommendations. To help stabilize a fabric item, insert T-shirt form or iron shiny side of freezer paper to wrong side of garment under area to be painted. Remove freezer paper when painting is complete.

Transferring Patterns:
Trace pattern onto tracing paper. Using removable tape, tape pattern to project. Place transfer paper coated-side down between project and tracing paper (using old transfer paper will help prevent smudges). If transferring pattern onto a dark surface, use light-colored transfer paper to transfer pattern.

Painting Basecoats:
A disposable plate makes a good palette. Use a medium round brush for large areas and a small round brush for small areas. Do not overload brush. Let paint dry between coats.

Transferring Details:
To transfer detail lines to design, reposition pattern and transfer paper over painted basecoats and use stylus or pencil to lightly draw over detail lines of design onto project.

Side Loading (shading or highlighting):
Dip one corner of a flat brush in water; blot on a paper towel. Dip dry corner of brush into paint. Stroke brush back and forth on palette until there is a gradual change from paint to water in each brush stroke. Stroke loaded side of brush along detail line on project, pulling brush toward you and turning project if necessary. For shading, side load brush with a darker color of paint. For highlighting, side load brush with lighter color of paint.

Line work:
To prevent smudging lines or ruining pen, let paint dry before beginning line work. Draw over detail lines with permanent pen.

Dots:
Dip the tip of a round paintbrush, the handle end of a paintbrush, or one end of a toothpick in paint and touch to project. Dip in paint each time for uniform dots.

Spatter Painting:
Dip bristle tips of a dry toothbrush into paint, blot on a paper towel to remove excess paint, then pull thumb across bristles to spatter paint on project.

Sponge Painting:
Use an assembly line method when making several sponge-painted projects. Place project on a covered work surface. Practice sponge-painting technique on scrap paper until desired look is achieved. Paint projects with first color and allow to dry before moving to next color. Use a clean sponge for each additional color.

For all over designs, dip a dampened sponge piece into paint; blot on a paper towel to remove excess paint. Use a light stamping motion to apply paint to project. Reapply paint to sponge as necessary.

For painting with sponge shapes, dip a dampened sponge shape into paint; blot on a paper towel to remove excess paint. Lightly press sponge onto project. Carefully lift sponge and allow to dry.

Sealing:
If a project will be handled frequently or used outdoors, we recommend sealing the item with clear sealer. Sealers are available in spray or brush-on form in a variety of finishes. Follow manufacturer's instructions to apply sealer.

EMBROIDERY STITCHES

BACKSTITCH
Referring to Fig. 1, bring needle up at 1; go down at 2. Bring needle up at 3 and pull through. For next stitch, insert needle at 1; bring up at 4 and pull through. Continue working to make a continuous line of stitches.

Fig. 1

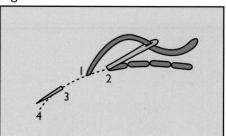

ADDING BEADS
Using a fine needle that will pass through bead, refer to project design and key for bead placement to sew bead in place. Bring needle up at 1, run needle through bead and then down at 2. Secure thread on back or move to next bead as shown in Fig. 2.

Fig. 2

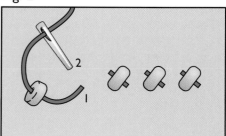

BLANKET STITCH

Bring needle up at 1. Keeping thread below point of needle, go down at 2 and up at 3 (Fig. 3). Continue working as shown in Fig. 4.

Fig. 3   Fig. 4

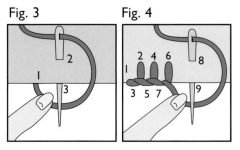

CROSS STITCH

Bring needle up at 1 and go down at 2. Come up at 3 and go down at 4 (Fig. 5).

Fig. 5

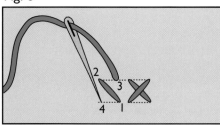

FRENCH KNOT

Bring needle up at 1. Wrap thread once around needle and insert needle at 2, holding thread with non-stitching fingers (Fig. 6). Holding thread until it must be released, tighten knot as close to fabric as possible while pulling needle back through fabric.

Fig. 6

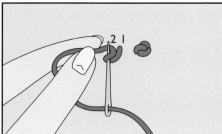

FEATHER STITCH

Bring needle up at 1; keeping thread below point of needle, go down at 2 and come up at 3 (Fig. 7). Go down at 4 and come up at 5 (Fig. 8). Continue working as shown in Fig. 9.

Fig. 7   Fig. 8

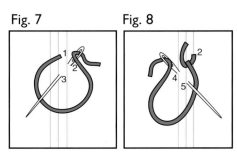

Fig. 9

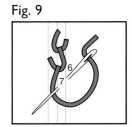

LAZY DAISY STITCH

Bring needle up at 1; take needle down again at 1 to form a loop and bring up at 2. Keeping loop below point of needle (Fig. 10), take needle down at 3 to anchor loop.

Fig. 10

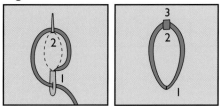

OVERCAST STITCH

Bring needle up at 1; take thread over edges of fabric and bring needle up at 2. Continue stitching along edges of fabric (Fig. 11).

Fig. 11

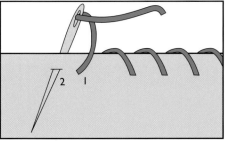

RUNNING STITCH

Referring to Fig. 12, make a series of straight stitches with stitch length equal to the space between stitches.

Fig. 12

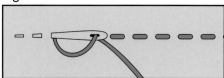

SATIN STITCH

Referring to Fig. 13, come up at odd numbers and go down at even numbers with the stitches touching but not overlapping.

Fig. 13

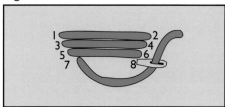

STEM STITCH

Referring to Fig. 14, come up at 1. Keeping thread below stitching line, go down at 2 and come up at 3. Go down at 4 and come up at 5.

Fig. 14

STRAIGHT STITCH

Bring needle up at 1 and take needle down at 2 (Fig. 15). Length of stitches may be varied as desired.

Fig. 15

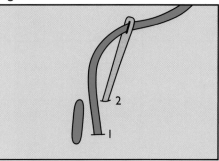

CROSS STITCH
COUNTED CROSS STITCH (X):
Work one Cross Stitch to correspond to each colored square in chart. For horizontal rows, work stitches in two journeys (Fig. 1).

Fig. 1

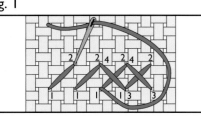

For vertical rows, complete each stitch as shown in Fig. 2.

Fig. 2

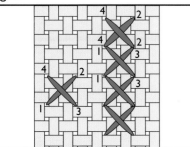

When the chart shows a Backstitch crossing a colored square (Fig. 3), work the Cross Stitch first, then work the Backstitch over the Cross Stitch.

Fig. 3

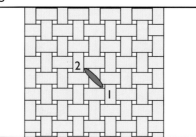

HALF STITCH (½X):
This stitch is one journey of the Cross Stitch and is worked from lower left to upper right (Fig. 4).

Fig. 4

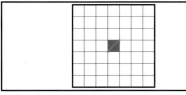

QUARTER STITCH (¼X):
Quarter Stitches are shown as triangular shapes of color in chart and color key. Come up at 1, then take needle down at 2 (Fig. 5).

Fig. 5

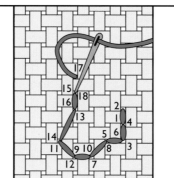

BACKSTITCH (B'ST):
For outline or details, Backstitch (shown in chart and color key by black or colored straight lines) should be worked after all Cross Stitch has been completed (Fig. 6).

Fig. 6

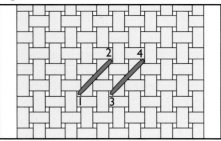

RECIPE INDEX

A

B

CREDITS

We want to extend a warm *thank you* to the generous people who allowed us to photograph our projects at their homes.

- *Earthly Grandeur:* Wes and Sue Ann Hall and Dan and Jeanne Spencer
- *Fruitful Opulence:* Shirley Held
- *Noble Estate:* Wes and Sue Ann Hall
- *Dreamy White Christmas:* Ellison Poe and Leighton Weeks
- *A Sterling Yuletide Tea:* Dan and Jeanne Spencer
- *Woodland Haven:* Becky Thompson
- *Reindeer Games:* Rhonda Fitz
- *Decorating Made Easy:* Charles and Peg Mills

To Magna IV Color Imaging of Little Rock, Arkansas, we say thank you for the superb color reproduction and excellent pre-press preparation.

Our sincere appreciation goes to photographers Nancy Nolan of Nola Studios; Ken West and Mark Mathews of Peerless Photography; and Jerry R. Davis of Jerry Davis Photography, all of Little Rock, Arkansas, for their excellent photography. Photography stylist Sondra Daniel also deserves a special mention for the high quality of her collaboration with these photographers.

To the talented people who helped in the creation of the following projects in this book, we extend a special word of thanks.

- *"A Peaceful Christmastide,"* page 40: Adapted for cross stitch by Carol Emmer
- *Silhouettes,* page 65: Paula Vaughan

We are sincerely grateful to the people who assisted in making and testing the projects in this book: Nelwyn D. Gray and Nora Faye Taylor.

Thanks also go to the people who collaborated with Oxmoor House on the food sections of this book: Kathleen Royal Phillips, who assisted with some of the recipes; photography stylists Melanie Clark and Connie Formby; and designers Alisa Hyde and Carol Tipton.